A Hebrew Text in Greek Dress

Dr. William V. McDonald is president of New Life Teaching Center, New Life Ministries, Inc. Based in Austin, TX, the organization is dedicated to bible research and education. He is an Associate Professor in the graduate School of Theology and Mission at Oral Roberts University – teaching Old Testament/Hebrew Scriptures courses. Dr. McDonald has over 30 years of experience in educational ministry teachings. He is the author of *You Are Free to Worry No More*. Visit the website at www.wmcdonaldministry.com.

A Hebrew Text in Greek Dress

A Comparison and Contrast Between

Jewish and Hellenistic Thought

William V. McDonald

New Life Teaching Center, New Life Ministries, Inc.
Austin, Texas

Designed by Sue Schoenfeld

Cover photo © Erica Guilane-Nachez, Fotolia.com

New Life Teaching Center, New Life Ministries, Inc.
www.wmcdonaldministry.com

Printed in the United States of America

CONTENTS

FORWARD

Most biblical scholars are trying to understand Scripture in a way that uncovers the message that the author intended to convey. We bring to the text our own presuppositions and pre-understandings. Our presuppositions deal with our attitude to the Scripture: Is the Bible God's Word? Is it true and trustworthy? These concepts will change from time to time in how we approach the Scripture. Our pre-understandings, however, are influenced by our training, what we have heard in Sunday school, and by our culture. Much of what we bring to the text may be wrong. It can distort our interpretation of the Bible. But pre-understanding can change with a more disciplined approach or with a better accumulation of knowledge.

Commonly held pre-understandings about the proper interpretation of biblical passages in the New Testament are being challenged by a group of scholars from the Jerusalem School of Synoptic Research. This school is made up of Jews and Christians who are interested in putting the New

Testament into its original Hebraic setting. Since most of the New Testament came from a Jewish-Christian background, it seems logical, therefore, to use the historical-cultural setting of the first century of the Christian era to better understand the meaning of that text.

The present volume attempts to do just that. William V. McDonald, a Ph.D. in Hebrew Studies from the University of Texas at Austin, applies the approach of the Jerusalem School to selected themes and passages in the Gospels. The idea that Aramaic was the primary language in use at the time of Jesus is challenged. His arguments are compelling that Hebrew was dominant and that there was a "parallel Hebrew culture existing side by side with that of the Hellenistic culture." It is this Hebrew culture that influenced the writers of the New Testament.

The concept of the Kingdom of Heaven is discussed in some detail. The present reality of the "Kingdom" is stressed. This is essential for a proper understanding of many of the sayings of Jesus. What Jesus was offering was an entrance into the kingdom, not in the future, but now. The kingdom is in this world. This kingdom existed before it appears in the Gospels.

The greater part of the book is devoted to a proper "Hebraic" understanding of the Beatitudes in Matthew 5:1-11. The author interacts with and takes issue with many outstanding scholars who have written commentaries on Matthew. These include: W. F. Albright and C. S. Mann, W. D. Davies and Dale D. Allison, Donald A. Hagner, Douglas R. A. Hare, and John Peter Lange. McDonald is convinced that too much emphasis has been placed by these scholars on the Hellenistic culture in the interpretation of the text. Approaching these same texts from a Semitic foundation unlocks fresh new understandings of the biblical material.

An Appendix gives brief information on some of the scholars who have contributed to a Semitic approach to New Testament studies.

Dr. Roy Hayden

PREFACE

It has been over sixty years since the findings of the Dead Sea Scrolls academic studies, which address the biblical text from a Hebraic perspective published their writings with a different historical approach about Christians during the Second Temple period. These authors are allowing us to view the Gospels through the lens of the original language of that day. This text rests on the assumptions that Hebrew was the spoken language of Jesus' day, not Greek or Aramaic, and that through the years recounted in the New Testament, strong Hebraic traditions continued to influence Christianity's development within the Hellenized culture of the Roman Empire. In view of recent historical evidence, there is no doubt that the language and culture before, during, and after Jesus' day were Hebraic or Mishnaic, and that there was a parallel Hebraic culture existing side by side with that of the Hellenistic culture, strong enough to influence those who translated and compiled the canonized text of our Gospels.

In this text, I pursue how these parallel cultures influenced the subsequent adaptations of the Gospels, as New Testament scholars were at pains to divorce the record of Jesus' early teaching from his Jewish roots and context, and to establish early Christian culture within the culture and political imperatives of the Roman Empire. First, I pursue a concept well known in Christian literature, "The Kingdom of Heaven," to show how the historical setting unlocks fresh new meanings of the text in which it appears. Hellenized reading of the passage stresses future promise and theology, while in the context of Jewish learning this concept referred mainly to community and political concerns of the day. Thereafter, I show how this concept helps to open a familiar set of passages from the Gospel according to Matthew, Chapter Five – the Beatitudes. Here, I contrast a reading informed by knowledge of the early Common Era's Jewish cultures with those offered by modern commentators who retain a Hellenistic vision of the era. The conclusion returns to the methodological process in which translations are used to carefully reflect specific translators' or commentators' ideologies.

INTRODUCTION

Since the discovery of the Dead Sea Scrolls, scholars have been rethinking their hypotheses concerning the original language of the Synoptic Gospels: "a revolution is taking place in our understanding of the New Testament. With the rebirth of Israel in 1947-1948 came the dramatic discovery of the Dead Sea Scrolls."[1] From the mid-twentieth and early twenty-first centuries, renowned scholars published innovative studies suggesting a Semitic foundation for interpreting the New Testament. These suggestions are based on research found in the Dead Sea Scrolls and other Jewish documents that indicate that the language of the people in Judea during the first century was Hebrew, not Greek or Aramaic as had been previously thought. These studies are currently providing scholars new insights into the Gospels, as well as the Epistles of Paul, Peter, James, and John.

While this most important finding of the Dead Sea Scrolls took place over sixty years ago, much of the evidence held within the historical sources remains undisclosed.[2] Many of the scholars who have been privileged to research and publish their works today are setting new standards in biblical research.[3]

The Dead Sea Scrolls along with other Jewish sources have opened new avenues in biblical hermeneutics today. The Hebrew genre has provided scholars such as William Sanford Lasor, Robert L. Lindsey, David Flusser, Shmuel Safrai, Roy B. Blizzard, Jr., Marvin Wilson, and Brad H. Young (see Appendix), opportunities to establish a strong foundation for their position of a Hebraic Gospel. Thus, each of these scholars has contributed important evidence supporting a Hebrew background of the New Testament.

What is less familiar about these scholars and their importance to the present project is their position in a long tradition of Christian scholarship: their willingness to go against two millennia of tradition that argues for an almost complete break between the Christian era and the Jewish culture in which these Hebraic events took place. These scholars, whose names have briefly been noted, run against the traditional Hellenistic perspective. Many of them work in the Jerusalem School of Synoptic Research and the Hebrew University. They are both Christian and Jewish scholars who are knowledgeable in biblical languages and have worked exclusively in Israel. These scholars have provided key information unfolding the cultural ties that millennia of exegetical habits have tried to erase. They read the Christian Bible, both Old and New Testament, as a text derived from the background of Semitic languages and cultures. Within the Semitic culture, the events and the stories of Jesus and his disciples were recorded. These stories tell how they lived as members of typical Jewish communities, and historically these communities experienced an unrelenting amount of pressure by the growing Roman Empire.

Because of the biblical writings produced by the founding members of The Jerusalem School of Synoptic

Research, a new generation of Old and New Testament scholars has emerged. They too are publishing articles and text books that are supporting a complete revision in reading Scripture from their Hebraic historical roots. Thus in this text I will examine two major themes found in the biblical text, "The Kingdom of Heaven," and "The Beatitudes of Matthew 5:1-11," to further establish a Hebraic perspective of the Gospels or the teachings of Jesus. The first chapter will examine the historical setting by providing examples of how a Hellenistic biased approach has obscured the real references of culture, habit, and politics in traditional Christian theology. It will be clear to see that what appears to be a reasonably self-evident term has in fact been obscured by ignoring the Hebrew terminology it rested upon and dismissing the kinds of community politics it referred to in Jewish communities. By working in this genre, I hope to extend the bridge built by the Jerusalem School of Synoptic Research and bring together sources that will give each reader access to the academic world of the New Testament's Semitic background.

The entire New Testament will not be examined, nor will all four Gospels, for such would be a task too extensive for this single study. Nor will this text attempt to invalidate what two millennia of Christian exegetes have done. Instead, I will focus on a set of key concepts and passages in order to emphasize the importance of Hebrew in studying the Gospels. My goal is thus straightforward: to illuminate the Hebraic roots of the Christian faith, and to show how problematic it is to interpret central concepts of Scripture only from a Hellenistic viewpoint. This examination will also clearly reveal how Hellenistic scholars simply overlooked the Semitic roots found in the Gospels. It is crucial to note that it is completely understandable how Christian exegetical traditions have from the beginning taken a Hellenistic approach to the textual materials of the first century.

My methodology is not new; such re-reading of Christian texts in light of new historical and philological data has been part of scholarly research since at least the era of Edward Pococke (1604-1691) who clearly wrote using a Semitic methodology for understanding textual materials. In *A Commentary on the Prophecy of Micah*, Pococke writes:

> For these and other reasons, even the care that the Jews themselves (as is by all known and confessed) always took of writing it exactly true, as that where on their own preservation depended, we cannot on any probable grounds question the integrity thereof. Yet a learned man, who is looked on to have laboured as much as any to question the integrity of the *Hebrew* text, doth confess that in Christ's time, and *Jonathans* the Parapharft, the Hebrew Books that they then had were the same that we now have. And what then have we further to be solicitous about in this matter? For of those was then the Book that our Saviour stood up to read in the Synagogue, and expounded by the same Spirit which first dedicated what was therein written. However these arguments may be eluded by such as will be contentious, yet they are such as may well sway a sober mind that neither before nor after Christ's time the Hebrew Copies were corrupted, and so ought to be our undoubted rule.[4]

Before the sixteenth and seventeenth centuries, and before the rise of the age of reasoning, men read the Bible and took what it said as the final authority on any subject about which it spoke. However, during the seventeenth and eighteenth centuries, various discoveries changed the mind of many concerning the Bible and other ancient literature. The invention of the telescope by Hans Lippershey, Galileo, and Hevelius allowed men to see worlds previously unknown. The invention of the microscope by Zacharias Janssen and Leeuwenhoek allowed others to view myriads of living creatures from a simple drop of pond water. During the nineteenth century, from 1831 to 1836, Charles Darwin sailed around the globe on the H.M.S. Beagle, postulating many of his theories as he was engrossed in experimentation and speculation of the time. Scientific laboratories were set up where studies in biology, chemistry, physiology, and psychological approaches emerged.

The age of speculation and skepticism became a model for investigating everything. Thus the Bible and the works of men like Herodotus, Manetho, Josephus, and Jerome did not escape this investigative approach. A move toward doubt and skepticism began to be made as early as the middle of the seventeenth century, and during the next two centuries skepticism concerning the Bible spread over the earth. Higher criticism became the vogue and one of the theories higher critics used was known as the "Documentary Hypothesis." Thus the historical dating of the Bible came under question by scholars during this time (the German School of exegesis).

In 1775, a French physician, Jean Astruc, began examining the Pentateuch in Hebrew and noted that in Genesis there were two names for God being used: *YHWH*, which was labeled as the "J" source; and *Elohim*, which was labeled as the "E" source. As a result of his study, Astruc stated that Genesis was written using a J and an E source. He also originally taught that Moses was not the author of the book. By 1781, John Eickhorn examined the entire Pentateuch and confirmed that Moses did write the text, again using the J and E sources. This crucial analysis of the Bible continued through the works of Alexander Geddes, 1773; Johann Vater, 1805; Willhelm DeWette, 1806/07; and Hermann Hupfeld, who offered the theory of the "four source hypothesis."

However, it was the work of Graf and Wellhausen (1865-1878) who stabilized the dating of authorship with the popular JEDP theory. These are some of the individuals who began the early critical investigation of the Bible.

W. F. Albright, in *Archaeological Discovery and the Scriptures*, writes that the discoveries of the "scrolls and fragments in the Jordan and Dead Sea valley since 1949 easily take precedence over all other finds except the tablets of Ugarit."[5] Albright goes on to state:

> They are clarifying intertestamental studies to an extent considered impossible only a few years ago. New Testament studies are being revolutionized as the date of the Gospels is pushed back and the meaning of obscure texts is illuminated. Neither "form criticism" in Bultmann's sense nor the popular "existential" interpretation of Paul and John can withstand the torrent of Jewish illustrative material in Hebrew and Aramaic – practically all antedating the Fall of Jerusalem in A.D. 70.[6]

According to Albright, the discovery of the Dead Sea Scrolls brought about a new era or a return to the time of Pococke when Hebrew was the standard used to analyze the Bible. Pococke states:

> The main thing in these Annotations endeavoured, is to settle the genuine and literal meaning of the Text. Seeing it is often very differently rendered by Interpreters, according to their different judgments, from what we read in our *English* Bibles; and that in them also we have various readings in the Margin, I have laboured as far as I could to find out the truth among them, by examining such as I have occasion to take notice of, by the Original

Hebrew, which is the standing rule which was at first by the goodness of God for such delivered to us by the Prophets and holy men divinely inspired, and hath ever since, by his wonderful Providence, been preserved uncorrupt and sincere.[7]

In Albright's illustration of translating a Hebrew word into Greek, he confirmed by doing so that the Hebrew word will open new interpretations within the text. He also stated that these "illustrations are so numerous in both the Old and the New Testament that it is scarcely necessary to belabor this point."[8] One final point by Albright, who in addressing the theory of Graf and Wellhausen, writes:

It has even been asserted recently that the Pentateuch was written by Moses in the exact form that has come down to us in the Hebrew Bible. So-called critical scholarship was partly responsible for this approach, since nineteenth-century critics insisted that the text of our printed Hebrew Bible had come down from the change. Today, thanks to the Dead Sea Scrolls, we know that this is not true. There were different recessions of the Pentateuch, and no immutable form can be attributed to any part of it. It is quite impossible to cut the Pentateuch up into patchwork of "JEP" with any hope of increasing our knowledge of what actually happened. That the Pentateuchal law is substantially Mosaic in origin and that patriarchal and Mosaic historical traditions are astonishingly early and dependable seems, in my opinion, certain.[9]

Much is at stake and much is being accomplished in the field of biblical criticism today. However, there is a great deal of resistance in seminaries and universities concerning their willingness to rethink cherished traditions held about the historical conditions which influenced the Judaic/Christian cultures from the time of Christ onward. For example, a conference was held December 14-17, 1992, on the Dead Sea Scrolls by the New Academy of Sciences, along with the Oriental Institute of the University of Chicago, to debate controversies concerning the scrolls. Scholars from Israel, Germany, Austria, Britain, Poland, Canada, and the United States gathered for four days, presenting academic papers questioning and defending theories centering on the Scrolls. One of the most notable debates focused on the controversial work of two noted scholars, Robert Eisenman and Michael Wise, who published *The Dead Sea Scrolls Uncovered: The First Complete Translation and Interpretation of 50 Key Documents Withheld for Over 35 Years.* A number of scholars argued that they "used other scholars' tedious and painstaking work of reconstruction for difficult manuscript readings, all the while claiming exclusive credit for the academic contributions originally made by other scholars."[10] The research of Michael Baigent and Richard Leigh in addressing the realities of the Scrolls published *The Dead Sea Scrolls Deception.* Their work has found its way into the libraries of many leading universities, thus thereby providing students with misleading conclusions based upon highly questionable sources. Baigent and Leigh's text "will be widely read because of the current interest in scroll research. Few in the scholarly world however, will take it seriously."[11] Nevertheless, the Dead Sea Scrolls have already provided, and will continue to provide, new evidence that the Bible is a different text from the one traditional scholarship has asserted.

To make the case how significant this transformation is for academic studies, the first chapter will outline briefly one example of what is at stake when we ignore the fact that the Christian Community today is embedded in Hellenism.

Thereby the first chapter will trace how the Gospels were adapted as part of the transformation of an original Semitic culture into a Hellenized culture that could only stand as part of the Roman Empire. Then, it will summarize briefly some of the major points made today about the culture that produced the Dead Sea Scrolls. That is, it will describe the community from which they originated and how these sources will lead the readers into a rich branch of current scholarship.

The next chapter will focus on the concept "Kingdom of Heaven" and how it emerged from the Hebrew Scriptures into the Gospels. The final chapters will compare and contrast The Beatitudes in Matthew, chapter 5:1-11, from a Greek to a Hebrew text that is beneath the canonized Greek manuscript. In each section an outline of significant doctrinal interpretations held by traditional and contemporary Christian scholars are examined. These positions, held by scholars who support a Hellenistic interpretation, will be compared and contrasted with sources found in Rabbinic Literature, connecting the roots of the Gospels with its natural source.

The conclusion will return to the general questions biblical scholars are asking today. These questions are similar to the kind posed by Ludwig Feuerbach a century and a half ago as he became confused with the understanding of the God of the Bible. Unlike Feuerbach, there is a growing group of scholars who are reading the Gospels from a Hebraic perspective. This allows these scholars to experience the words of the Gospels in a manner akin to that of the original audiences who saw and heard it for themselves. This approach does challenge what traditional Church authorities asserted. And yet it is a much more significant approach to reading the text, which confers more historical authority in Christian and Judaic scholarship alike. This approach will also stress critical thinking and multicultural research rather than simple individual interpretive readings alone.

NOTES FOR INTRODUCTION

[1]David Bivin and Roy Blizzard, Jr., *Understanding the Difficult Words of Jesus* (Shippensburg, PA: Destiny Image Publishers, 1983) p. 17: "These priceless, ancient manuscripts, followed a few years later by the discovery of the Bar-cochba letters, became vital contributions to a fuller understanding of the New Testament writings. Many scholars in Israel are now convinced that the spoken and written language of the Jews in the Land of Israel at the time of Jesus was indeed Hebrew; and that the Synoptic Gospels were derived from original Hebrew sources. These scholars, fluent in both Greek and Hebrew, have proposed impressive solutions to major problems of the New Testament interpretation. Important discoveries which they have made serve to illuminate the very Hebraic style of speech used by Jesus and his first followers, and to make possible a more accurate translation of the Gospels."

[2]Theodor H. Gaster, *The Dead Sea Scriptures in English Translation with Introduction and Notes* (New York, London: Anchor Books Doubleday, 1956) pp xv-xvi: "The scholarly literature on the Scrolls increases from day to day, and much that was at first obscure is gradually becoming clear. On the other hand, varying theories and 'reconstruction,' often premature and fantastic, still abound, and there is a crying need for the interpretation of the texts to be both 'de-mythologized' and de-sensationalized."

[3]Robert L. Lindsey, *A Hebrew Translation of the Gospel of Mark: Greek-Hebrew Diglot with English Introduction* (Jerusalem: Dugith Publishers Baptist House, 1969) p. 9. "Some years ago I came to the conclusion that a new Hebrew translation of the New Testament was badly needed. In 1951 with the aid of a couple of Israeli translators who worked from English and French texts, I completed a preliminary trial translation. It was however not until 1959 that I was able to begin the necessary research for this later stage. I chose the Gospel of Mark under the impression that it was the first of our Gospels and contained the kind of simple Greek text which would make translating relatively easy...Rather to my surprise the preliminary study of the Greek text of Mark turned up the conclusion that the Greek word order and idiom was more like Hebrew than literary Greek. This gave me the frightening feeling that I was as much in the process of 'restoring' the original Hebrew work as in that of creating a new one, like many a Semitics student before me, as I wondered if the Gospel might not be a literal translation from some Semitic original."

[4]Edward Pococke, *A Commentary on the Prophecy of Micah* (London: The University of Oxford, 1676) p. unnumbered preface.

[5]William F. Albright, "Archaeological Discovery and the Scriptures," Vol XXII, No. 19, *Christianity Today* June 21, 1968, p. 4.

[6]Albright, p. 4: "In dealing with the Bible from the standpoint of modern archaeological discovery, one must remember that the Bible is both divine, since it rests on divine inspiration, and human, since it has come to us through human channels. Much of both the Old and New Testaments was transmitted by oral tradition. In other words, the Bible contains many things handed down by word of mouth – in the Old Testament largely in verse and in the New Testament as oral reports of works and acts of Jesus and his disciples. The written text of these early traditions followed later – though earlier than supposed by 'critical' scholars."

[7]Pococke, p. preface.

[8]Albright, p. 4: "In studying the new Testament, we now have a similar increase in the quantity of Semitic texts dating to just before and just after the time of Christ. They vastly increase our understanding of the grammar and vocabulary of the Hebrew and Aramaic spoken and written in the time of Christ. For the first time we can really grasp the significance of the Syriac versions of the Gospels."

[9]Albright, p. 5.

[10]Brad H. Young, Dead Sea Scrolls Conference, Vol. 7 number 2 (Austin TX: Yavo Digest) p. 17: "The discovery of the Dead Sea Scrolls has stirred up controversy and conflict. The start of the conference reflected this 'present reality' when it became apparent that 11 of the prestigious scroll scholars had canceled their lectures due to the publication of a very controversial new book by Robert Eisenman and Michael Wise...Their basic assertion, moreover, that for the most part these 50 scrolls had never been published before, was indeed greatly exaggerated."

[11]Brad H. Young, "The Dead Sea Scrolls Deception" Article Vol. 6 number 2 (Austin TX: Yavo Digest) p. 18: "The method of research used in the book is quite disturbing because the authors are so selective in their discussion of the evidence. They pick and choose what suits their purposes. The authors present three major divisions in their treatment of the alleged Dead Sea Scrolls cover-up. "I. The Deception, II. The Vatican's Representatives and III. The Dead Sea Scrolls."

CHAPTER 1

THE HISTORICAL ROOTS OF HELLENISM IN

CHRISTIANITY

The historical bases which lead to obscuring the teachings of Jesus in the Gospels were found in Hellenism and not the Semitic culture of His day. An examination of both Hellenistic and Jewish culture for the purpose of understanding what forces were at work in the development of early Christian traditions/teachings is imperative. Thus a brief overview of the Dead Sea Scroll scholarship, as it relates to these influences within Christian culture and how they are understood within the community today. Finally this chapter will also suggest that a concept like "The Kingdom of Heaven," which was believed to be a particularly difficult one to recoup when moving texts like the Gospels between their Semitic roots, and the new Hellenized culture in which they were to function, can now be more clearly understood.

The First Years: History and Doctrine

Why did the early church embrace Hellenism, in view of

their historical roots in Judaism? Part of this answer begins three hundred years before the birth of Jesus with Alexander the Great. This shift has traditionally been summarized as follows:

> Alexander the Great conquered the Persian Empire, and with it Palestine and Jerusalem. After his death, his generals created independent kingdoms in Egypt and Syria, which fought continually for control of Palestine. During this period, Greek culture and language, known as Hellenism, were superimposed on the region. The Bible was translated into Greek (the Septuagint), the language of most Jews outside Palestine, and Jews grappled with the benefits and threats of the influences of this foreign culture. Large numbers of Jews, either by force or by choice, settled in Alexandria, Egypt, and in many cities in Greece and the Mediterranean, which resulted in a Diaspora.[12]

The Jews were under Greco-Roman influence for over three hundred years. This shift was, by early standards, severe. Palestine was ruled by the Ptolemies of Egypt, and by 200 B.C.E. the Seleucid Antiochus III of Syria had conquered Palestine. By 175 B.C.E. the Hellenization of Jerusalem itself began under the high priests Jason and Menelaus. A group of "Hellenizers seem to have imagined a kind of syncretism of Judaism and Greek religion, such as was common at that time."[13] In 166 B.C.E. the first of many revolts began with the priest Mattathias. This was also known as the Maccabean revolt, which was the first of several important revolts that spanned a period of three hundred years. This marked the rebirth of a distinct Semitic culture within the Greco-Roman world.[14]

When Mattathias and his friends learned of it, they mourned for them deeply. And each said to his neighbor: "If we all do as our brethren have done and refuse to fight with the Gentiles for our lives and our ordinances, they will quickly destroy us from the earth." So they made this decision that day: "Let us fight against every man who comes to attack us on the Sabbath day: let us not all die as our brethren died in their hiding places."[15]

The Hasidim made up the majority of the Maccabaen army. They fought to restore religious freedom that had existed under the charter of Antiochus III. During the first stage of one of the most important revolts the Hasidim and Judas Maccabaeus fought together. Only the Maccabaeans fought for complete political independence from the beginning. Their army was split after the successors of Antiochus IV appointed Eliakim (Alcimus) as high priest. The Hasidim believed their goal of religious freedom had been met; therefore they accepted the new high priest. The Maccabaeus family left Jerusalem and retreated into the mountains of Gophna. Their mistrust of the new high priest was soon proven correct, as "it became clear that Eliakim could not or would not give up his Hellenizing ways."[16]

The Bible was then adapted as part of these political shifts. In the third century B.C.E. the Hebrew Bible was translated into Greek.[17] This translation was designed to help the Jewish population of the Diaspora who spoke Greek as their primary language. By the first century B.C.E., Jews could be found everywhere within the Roman Empire. They were in Palestine, Syria, Egypt, North Africa, Greece, Italy, as well as Spain and Gaul, and throughout the Parthian Empire, including Babylon and the cities of Nehardea, Nisibis, Persia, Media, Elam, Seleucia on the Tigris River, and other surrounding countries.[18]

In spite of this heavy Greek influence, the Jews managed to maintain their distinct identity as a cultural and religious group, and with that identity they survived as a people. In many ways their survival was based upon the Jews' unique religious system, and on the particular toleration granted them by the Roman Empire. The Sages, in the home land of Israel, recognized the possible extinction of their faith, if nothing was done about the growing population of non-Hebrew speaking Jews in the Diasporas. Their solution was to translate the Torah into Greek, thus the legend of the Seventy. The Septuagint was not a confirmation of Hellenism. It was, however, an adaptation for the survival of their religion. Out of that unique religious system arose early Christianity, which began as a sect of Judaism but shortly thereafter amalgamated an even more Greco-Roman religious element into it. By the fourth century C.E., after a long period of persecution, Christianity would become the official religion of the Roman Empire, and emerge as the dominant religion of western culture, as it remains even to this day.[19]

What is crucial to remember is that, at the dawn of Jesus' movement, he was a faithful Jew, as were his disciples and their followers who resided in Palestine. They "studied the Torah and were strict in their observance of the commandments."[20] Their dress and speech reflected community norms of the Jewish Diaspora in the Roman Empire. During this early period of Christianity, several different groups of Christians began to establish their identity to which they were part of, yet distinct within, the non-Roman communities of the Empire. Among those groups were Jewish Christians, Non-Jewish/Christians, and Ebionite Christians, the latter of which sprang from the Jewish Christian followers.[21] A doctrinal point served to distinguish these groups from each other: the Non-Jewish Christians regarded Jesus as a great Prophet, but also as the Messiah; Jesus' resurrection as that Messiah formed the cornerstone of their faith.

The historical existence of these various groups is not to be doubted: "The Jewish Christians are known to us not only from the New Testament but also from some Christian Apocrypha."[22] Moreover, they have left many traces:

> Professor Shlomo Pines has discovered an early source in an Arabic adaptation made in the tenth century which proves that the last groups of such Jewish Christians were still in existence in the tenth century C.E. One can detect traces of their principal beliefs and even discover whole works of theirs in an adapted form in Christian literature of the period of the new Testament onward. The Jewish Christians interpreted the issues of Christianity in their own way and according to their own traditions and information. It is clear that some of their materials, adapted to suit the interests of the Church, have penetrated into the ecclesiastical literature of Gentile Christianity. These Jewish Christians were persecuted by the Church and regarded as infidels and heretics who had gone the wrong way and had attempted to Judaize Christianity. It was said of them that their world-view was deficient, and that they did not comprehend the divinity of Jesus.[23]

The Ebionites, who also embraced Christianity, held different views from the other two groups. They were vegetarians with a belief in opposition to the practice of sacrifices. They believed that the Jews were commanded to offer sacrifices as punishment for the event at Sinai. Out of the Ebionites came a peculiar prophetic sect, the Manicheans, who existed around one hundred C.E. in

Mesopotamia. It was inevitable that, of these many Christian groups, one would come to dominate: "Around the year 200 C.E. the Manichean religion was a serious candidate for the position of a world religion."[24] For a while, the Church Father Augustine became a follower of Manicheanism, as this religion moved across the land.

Despite these differences in dogma, Jewish-Christians still shared much as part of a single cultural group and as part of the Roman Empire. The first two hundred years, for example, much, if not all, of the religious order of the Church was taken from the practices found in the synagogue. The one common area held by both Jewish Christians and Non-Jewish Christians was their persecution by the Roman Empire. It was not their own theological positions that brought about their persecution; rather, it was their increasingly divergent position as potential citizens of Rome that led to their persecution. They failed to recognize the divinity of the emperor or showed disloyalty by not swearing to the gods of the state.

The groups nonetheless demonstrated increasing awareness of their own theological differences, which are documented in a series of councils. One of the first was the Council of Jerusalem, convened in 50 C.E. This council was made up of Jewish Christians only, and "it consisted not of the apostles alone, but of apostles, elders, and brethren. We know that Peter, Paul, John, Barnabas, and Titus were present, perhaps all the other apostles."[25]

These councils document first and foremost that the Jewish community was aware of its changing position within the empire. The Jerusalem Council of Jewish Christians were suspicious of Paul because he accepted Gentiles into the community of faith so easily. Still, they ruled that the many aspects of law should not be imposed upon these new non Jews becoming converts. By the time of the Roman Wars, "the Jewish Christian groups immigrated to Pella across the Jordan, and later they returned to Jerusalem."[26] That solution was not universally applauded: after the Second Jewish Revolt, non Jewish Christians did not permit Jewish Christians to reside within Jerusalem. Their reason was simple: these Jewish Christians were Jews and thus associated with the Jewish community at large. This same group of Jewish Christians later fled to Lebanon.

Because of such early disputes, a type of persecution developed between Jewish and non Jewish Christians. Jewish Christians were persecuted as heretics from the second century onward, and Christianity forbade them from keeping the commandments: "The Jewish Christians were reminded of their Judaism and began to feel an increasing sense of identification with the people of Israel."[27] One of the most important facts passed on by these Jewish Christians was their position, "that the proper language of teaching, in which the early Gospels had been written, was Hebrew, and that, when the Gospels had been translated into other languages it was as though they had been forged."[28] A major factor that produced the eventual final split between these groups was recorded in the writings of Flusser, who writes:

> The Jewish Christians were rejected by the Jews and persecuted by the Christians, who regarded them as heretics and villains. Despite all this, Christian literature reflects their creative vitality and their loyalty to Judaism. Because of ecclesiastical censorship, only some relics of their own writings have reached us. But the faithfulness of the Jewish Christians to Judaism, despite all their difficulties, is worthy of admiration.[29]

He, therefore, acknowledges that the split between the two groups as two separate religions was by no means completed in the first two centuries after Jesus.

Nonetheless, the Jewish Christians were inexorably moving towards a more Hellenistic identification with the Empire and a Greco-Roman cultural legacy, while the Jews were identifying more and more with Hebrew and Israel. An important historical event that influenced the early believers in selecting Hellenism over Judaism was the Bar Kokhba revolt. The Roman Empire was becoming increasingly expansionist and interested in enforcing a uniform lifestyle in its provinces:

> During the second Jewish war the stage was set for a third rebellion, the revolt of Bar Kokhba in 132-135. The latter was even more devastating to Judea than the war of 66-70 C.E. and was perhaps the worst single catastrophe for the Jewish people until the Holocaust. When Hadrian succeeded to the throne, he at first pursued a policy of reconciliation and restoration in the provinces. Destroyed cities were rebuilt, and Hadrian even considered allowing the Jews to rebuild the temple in Jerusalem. However, he soon changed his mind, perhaps because of his tendencies to want to Hellenize his empire. He came to hate foreign religions, and went so far as to forbid castration, which was interpreted to include circumcision. This was a strike at the very heart of Jewish identity and religion. It is uncertain whether this decree was made before or after the war. The spark that ignited the revolt was Hadrian's decision in 130 C.E., to build a pagan city, Aelia Capitolina, on the site of Jerusalem.[30]

The Roman Emperor Hadrian banned Jewish circumcision throughout the Empire under penalty of death. The Jews of Israel were further outraged by the Emperor's intention to rebuild Jerusalem as a Roman city with pagan temples, including a temple to Jupiter on the site of the Jewish temple. It was clear Rome was aware that these measures would provoke the Jews. Nevertheless, the Empire was completely unprepared for the events that were to come.

Unlike the Jewish War, this revolt was carefully planned. Jews in different parts of the Diaspora gave funds secretly, and fortifications were built and arms collected with hopes of defeating the military might of Rome.[31] The Jews were unified under one military commander; his name was Bar Kokhba, son of the star, in Greek or Latin translations. Because of the discovery of the Bar Kokhba letters, scholars are certain about the details of this leader.[32] His actual name was Shim'on Bar Kokhba; however, during the war his name was slightly changed because of a popular Bible passage in Numbers 24:17: "there shall come forth a star [Kokhba] out of Jacob." Thus, Rabbi Akiva, one of the leading sages of his day, declared Bar Kokhba to be the long awaited historical king messiah.

At this point, the newer historical record comes into play, showing that theological positions had distinct political overtones within the empire. To further establish Rabbi Akiva's beliefs, and to join a distinct political movement with the theological cause, the new leader adopted this title "Nasi," prince of Israel. According to the Dead Sea Scrolls and rabbinic literature, this title belonged to the coming Messiah.[33] Bar Kokhba proved to be a capable leader who defeated two Roman legions, the tenth and the sixth that were stationed in Judea. In 132 C.E., Bar Kokhba swiftly took control of Jerusalem and parts of Judea. As leader, "he issued coins proclaiming 'Year One of the Redemption of Israel' and 'For the freedom of Jerusalem.'"[34] In taking on this power, the Jews were directly challenging the power of the Roman state. Indeed, they were openly in opposition to Hadrian's Hellenizing program.

This political opposition helped divide Jewish Christians from Jews proper. Historians recorded that the whole of the Roman Empire might have toppled if the Parthian kingdom had joined the revolt. It is clear that, had not Rome reacted fast and swiftly with a full force against the Jewish revolts, Rome would have fallen. By 134-135 C.E., the Romans were at full strength, with twelve legions that numbered about 120,000 men. At Betar, in August 135 C.E., Bar-Kokhba was killed. Remnants of his followers hid for several years in caves in the Judean desert where the Bar-Kokhba letters were found. The lesson was not lost on the non-Jewish Christian community, which saw and heard how the Romans crushed the revolt and dealt harshly with the Jewish population. According to historians, 580,000 Jews died fighting, and others were hunted down and executed. The Romans destroyed 50 fortresses and 985 towns and villages: "Nearly the entire land of Judea was laid waste. The world's slave markets were glutted with Hebrew slaves, whose price fell to less than a horse's feed."[35]

Not surprisingly, the Emperor Hadrian began a religious persecution of Jews by outlawing the teaching of the Torah. This persecution ended when Hadrian died in 138 C.E. The destruction of the temple and the persecution of the Jews had an interesting effect on the Gentile Church, which now had cause to disavow Judaism as anything other than an ancestor of their own religion:

> It was the greatest calamity of Judaism and a great benefit to Christianity; a refutation of the one, a vindication and emancipation of the other. It not only gave a mighty impulse to faith, but at the same time formed a proper epoch in the history of the relation between the two religious bodies. It separated them forever.

Henceforth the heathen could no longer look upon Christianity as a mere sect of Judaism, but must regard and treat it as a new, peculiar religion. The destruction of Jerusalem, therefore, marked that momentous crisis at which the Christian church as a whole burst forth forever from the chrysalis of Judaism, awoke to a sense of its maturity, and in government and worship at once took its independent stand before the world.[36]

The rise of Christianity thus became one of the most important events in the history of Judaism, as part of the believing community turned away from the Empire that had originally sponsored it. The Christianity that had begun as a sect of Judaism and shortly amalgamated Greco-Roman religious elements into it had now established an independent identity. By the fourth century C.E. it had become the official religion of the Roman Empire, and the dominant religion of Western culture to this day.

To be sure, from 137 to 325, the Christian Church still faced persecution under different emperors. Justin Martyr of 165 records important information concerning the history of the Church and its practices. By "the third century 202 C.E. Septimius Severus, turned perhaps by Montanitic excesses, enacted a rigid law against the further spread both of Christianity and of Judaism."[37] Decius Trajan (249-251) continued the harsh persecution of the Church and resolved to root out all atheistic and seditious sects.

The new Church's triumph was soon to come. In 306, C.E. Constantine became emperor of Gaul, Spain, and Britain. Constantine quickly began to restore religious tolerances to the Church. It was an edict issued in 311 by Constantine that "prepared the way for the legal recognition of Christianity, as the religion of the empire."[38] At the end of his life, it is recorded that:

The Roman emperor Constantine converted to Christianity on his deathbed in 337 C.E., and within a few decades Christianity was to become the official religion of the Roman Empire. Henceforth, much of the world's Jewish population would live under Christian rule, discriminated against and reviled as a stiff-necked people who were the killers of Christ, yet must be tolerated to bear witness to the truth of Christianity.[39]

The Council of Nicaea in 323 C.E. took the first step in establishing Christianity as the official religion of the Roman Empire. The councils, also known as the Synods, first appeared around 264-269 C.E. in Spain with the Council of Elvira. Schaff records, "there are several kinds of Synods according to their size, Diocesan, Provincial (or Metropolitan), National, Patriarchal, and ecumenical (or Universal)."[40] Constantine inaugurated the Council of Nicaea in 325 C.E. as the first celebrated council with legal state authority to issue rulings concerning spiritual matters.

The Synodical system consolidated the Christian Church out of what had been independent communities held together by faith; they became a powerful confederation within the political organization of the Roman Empire. The Synodical system of government claimed their authority reached back to the Council of Jerusalem: "In which all classes of the Christian community are represented in the management of public affairs and in settling controversies respecting faith and discipline."[41] Nonetheless, there was a hundred and twenty year span between the Jerusalem Council and the start of the Synod system.

The difference between the first Council and the first Synod is critical in marking the moment when the Christian Church emerged clearly and distinct from the Jews of the Roman Empire. The Jerusalem Council had been made up of all Jews, who dealt with the question of what they were going to do with all the non-Jews coming into the faith. According to historical records just a little over one century later, there were no Jews among the Synod Council: "The Greek and Roman Churches gradually departed from the apostolic polity and excluded not only the laity, but also the lower clergy from all participation in the legislative councils. The decree which it passed and the pastoral letter which it sent, are the first in the long line of decrees and canons and encyclicals which issued from ecclesiastical authorities."[42] That is, these documents record Christianity as a self-aware religion instead of a collection of diverse communities.

What today's Hellenistic modern scholars tend to overlook is the obvious continuity that runs underneath this break; the Church Fathers who preceded this period were, necessarily, highly influenced by the conditions of early Church history of the first, second, and third centuries. However, Philip Schaff, in his eight-volume collection, *The History of the Christian Church*, injects his personal interpretation concerning Church history during the period of 66 to 100 C.E. Under the heading, "The Central Idea," Schaff shifts from recording the chronology of Church history to injecting his personal interpretation of the events of that time. He thus leaves the impression for the reader to accept his interpretation as a clear depiction of the historical events of that day.

Nothing can be further from the truth. The Jews, the Christian Jews, and the non-Jewish Christians did not simply break because of theological differences, as stated by Schaff. His text promotes an interpretation that encouraged the reader to view the Jewish and non-Jewish Christian harmony as being destroyed because of theological reasons:

> First of all, God has a sovereign right over all
> his creatures and manifests both his mercy and

his righteousness in the successive stages of the historical execution of his wise designs. His promise has not failed, for it was not given to all the carnal descendants of Abraham and Isaac, but only to the spiritual descendants, the true Israelites who have the faith of Abraham, and they have been saved, as individual Jews are saved to this day. And even in his relation to the vessels of wrath who by unbelief and ingratitude have fitted themselves for destruction, he shows his longsuffering. In the next place, **the real cause of the rejection of the body of Jews is their own rejection of Christ. They sought their own righteousness by works of the law instead of accepting the righteousness of God by faith**. Finally, the rejection of the Jews is only temporary and incidental in the great drama of history. It is overruled for the speedier conversion of the Gentiles, and the conversion of the full number or the organic totality of the Gentiles (not all individual Gentiles) will lead ultimately to the conversion of Israel. A hardening in part has befallen Israel, until the fullness of the Gentiles be come in; and so all Israel shall be saved.[43]

This statement does indeed convey a sense of the rhetoric that was at play in the division of two religious groups. Yet it deliberately elides what "hardening has befallen Israel." It refers to a resistance to the Roman Empire, not to the emerging Christian principle *per se*.

Subsequent to this political situation, however, the rhetoric did not change. The future of Christians was discussed within Church circles as if it were only a theological force, with few, if any, references to the Church – external forces that made the theological decisions necessary to the survival of the community. The Synod of Elvira (306 C.E.) was exemplary. It was a Synod that, possibly, was attended by nineteen bishops and twenty-six presbyters who came from the Southern districts of Spain. They produced canons of Church law that brought about more misinterpretations between Jewish Christians and non-Jewish Christians. Eighty-one Latin canons were passed in favor of church discipline and austere morals. Thirty-six of the eighty-one canons, for example, prohibit the admission of sacred pictures in church buildings, "while the Roman Catholic writers explain it either as prohibition of representations of the deity only, or as a prudential measure against heathen desecration of holy things."[44] Despite their clear theological content, such prohibitions also clearly reflect changes in lifestyle that accompanied further shifts toward Hellenistic, Greco-Roman norms of behavior and a moving away from the Middle Eastern, Semitic norms out of which the early Church had emerged.

NOTES FOR CHAPTER 1

[12]Naomi Pasachoff and Robert J. Littman, *Jewish History in 100 Nutshells* (Northvale, New Jersey, London: Jason Aronson Inc., 1943) p. 49.

[13]M. Avi-Yonah, *The Jews under Roman and Byzantine Rule* (Jerusalem: The Magnes Press, The Hebrew University, 1984) p. 3: "Most of the oriental nations living under Hellenistic monarchies on the political plane appreciated Greek culture. Such Hellenization seemed to the Greeks a natural process, because in their eyes the Orientals were barbarians without cultural values of their own. Starting from these mistaken premises, Antiochus IV tried to establish Greek culture and religion in Judaea by force."

[14]Helmut Koester, *Introduction to the New Testament: History, Culture and Religion of the Hellenistic Age* (Berlin, New York: Walter De Gruyter, 1962) pp. 211-212: "The turning point was the expulsion of Jason, who, though a member of the reform party, was still a

legitimate Zadokite and thus even for the conservatives a guarantor of the "laws of the father." However, in 172 BCE, Menelaus, the brother of an officer of the temple named Simon, took Jason's place...Only now did the situation reach a crisis point."

[15]Bruce M. Metzger, *The Apocrypha of the Old Testament* (New York: Oxford University Press, 1957) p. 225: "Then there united with them a company of Hasideans, mighty warriors of Israel, every one who offered himself willingly for the law. And all who became fugitives to escape their troubles joined them and reinforced them."

[16]Avi-Yonah p. 4: "On the contrary, he seems to have supported religious assimilation, for instance by breaking down the balustrade which prevented Gentiles from entering the Inner Temple. When the local Greek commander, Nicanor, openly threatened the Temple and its priests, even the Hasidim had to admit that there could be no sure hope of religious freedom under foreign rule. This was the moment when the Jewish nation opted for political freedom. Although the battle continued for many years, the decision to seek freedom was taken once and for all and could not be reversed."

[17]Koester, pp. 252-253: "The term 'Septuagint' (LXX) designates the Greek translation of the Old Testament."

[18]Pasachoff and Littman, p. 67.

[19]Pasachoff and Littman, p. 68.

[20]David Flusser, *Jewish Sources in Early Christianity* (New York: Adama Books, 1987) p. 81: also Flusser, p. 73: "The Jews of the Hebrew-speaking Diaspora were a factor which exercised some influence on the transformation of Christianity into a religion of the Gentiles. These Jews spoke Greek, and their literary creation was in Greek. In those days a sense of the emptiness of polytheistic beliefs and of the moral corruption of mankind was widespread throughout the world, and there was a

growing sympathy for the Jews and for their attitude to religion. Many people joined Judaism as full proselytes, and others, who were called 'God-fearing,' did not take upon themselves the full yoke of the Commandments, but undertook to keep some of the obligations of Judaism. Such men were the first to join Christianity as a result of the preaching of Paul and his sect."

[21] Flusser, p. 125.

[22] Flusser, p. 82.

[23] Flusser, p. 82.

[24] Flusser, p. 86: "This religion had spread from North Africa to India. Its founder was Mani, who lived in Persia under the Sassanid King Sapor I. His father, Patak, was for many years a member, together with his son, of the Erchasaite sect, whose ideas exercised an influence on the Manichean religion."

[25] Philip Schaff, *History of the Christian Church*, Vol. I (Grand Rapids Michigan: Wm. B. Eerdmans Publishing Company, 1910) p. 503.

[26] Flusser, p. 87.

[27] Flusser, p. 87: "They claimed that Paul, Peter, and even James had been driven by an instinct for power, and therefore had adapted themselves to ways of the Gentiles. They criticized the three in the same manner as later Jewish literature, maintaining that because of Christianity's turning towards the Gentiles due to impure motives, it had lost the chance of being accepted by the Jews. Unlike the Gentile Christians, who faced east in their prayers, the Jewish Christians continued to face the ruined Temple in the Holy City of Jerusalem."

[28] Flusser, p. 88.

[29] Flusser, p. 88.

[30] Pasachoff and Littman, p. 96.

[31] Hershel Shanks, *Christianity and Rabbinic Judaism: A Parallel History of Their Origins and Early*

Development (Washington, D.C.: Biblical Archaeology Society, 1992) p. 127.

[32]Marvin R. Wilson, *Our Father Abraham: Jewish Roots of the Christian Faith* (Grand Rapids, Michigan: William B. Eerdmans Publishing Company, 1973) p. 82: "As they had in the First Jewish Revolt, the Jewish Christians refused to fight. Failure to assist their countrymen in this final ill-fated drive for national independence alienated them even further from the Jewish community. It also left them more vulnerable to persecution. A second factor which created a significant wedge between the two groups centered on Bar Kokhba. The Jewish Christians had but one Messiah, the risen Jesus of Nazareth, who could command their allegiance. Their loyalty could not be directed to both Yeshua (Jesus) and Simon. Thus commitment to the cause of Bar Kokhba may have 'virtually meant a denial of the Messiahship of Jesus.'"

[33]Pasachoff and Littman, p. 95.

[34]Pasachoff and Littman, p. 95: "Although Jews were spread throughout the Roman Empire, there was unrest among them. This unrest was brought to a head during the rule of the Roman Emperor Trajan (reigned 98-117 C.E.) In an attempt to expand the empire, Trajan became involved in a war with the Parthians, who dominated in Babylon and Persia. At first successful, Trajan expanded the limits of the empire with his conquest of Armenia and northern Mesopotamia, including Adiabene, the rulers of which had converted to Judaism. However, while in the midst of this war, the Jews of Cyrenaica, Egypt, and Cyprus revolted in 115 C.E. This rebellion spread to Judea, particularly to Galilee, but was apparently not too widespread there."

[35]Pasachoff and Littman, p. 97: "One of the victims of this persecution was Hananiah ben Teradyon. When

arrested Hananiah admitted that he taught the Torah because it was God's will. The Romans sentenced him to be burned at the stake, his wife to be executed, and his daughter to be sold into a brothel. The Romans wrapped him in the scroll of Torah, which he had with him when he was arrested, and put him on a pyre of green brushwood. His chest covered with water to slow the burning."

[36]Schaff, vol. I, pp 403-404.

[37].chaff, Vol. II, p. 57.

[38]Schaff, Vol. II, p. 72.

[39]Pasachoff and Littman, p. 102.

[40]Schaff, Vol. II. P. 176.

[41]Schaff, Vol. I, p. 504.

[42]Schaff, Vol. I, p. 504.

[43]Schaff, Vol. I, p. 540.

[44]Schaff, Vol. II. P 180: "Otherwise the Synod is thoroughly catholic in spirit and tone. Another characteristic feature is the severity against the Jews who were numerous in Spain. Christians are forbidden to marry Jews."

CHAPTER 2

THE HELLENISTIC AGE: SCHOLARS AND THE

HELLENIZATION MYTH

It is important to point out that only a cursory look at Church history under the Roman Empire has been given. However, one should not overlook the second largest influence in Christianity that emerged within the Church... the Greek culture of Asia Minor...and how it was in full play in the Mediterranean. History has recorded how a political legacy changed a religion, and how these changes influenced scholars who evaluated the cultural legacy of the region: Hellenism, which was an allegiance to the legacy of ancient Greece.

History supports the view that Jews and Christian Jews lived and functioned in the Roman Empire within a Hellenized environment. By the tenth century immigrants from Ionia and Aeolis had already settled along the coast of Asia Minor. Cities like Smyma, Ephesus, Priene, Mysus, and Miletus were founded by the rulers of the Lydian kings of the Greek culture of the Mediterranean areas. As they retained their power as an Eastern culture, their influence contributed to the process of Hellenization in Asia Minor. A split began to emerge between the Jewish Christians and the non Jewish Christians. The colonies under this newly founded culture first produced economic growth, marked by the opening of new markets in exports.[45] Yet the development of Greek culture brought about the beginning of the intellectual age that continued within the Rome period.

While the Romans experienced many conflicts, their great strength allowed them to dominate the eastern part of the Mediterranean, with Persian influence gradually replacing the rule of Lydian kings in Asia Minor prior to the fourth century. Eventually, the Persians conquered Syria, Egypt, Asia Minor, and Greece. However, their amalgamation of the Greeks homeland did not succeed.[46] The political, cultural, and economical influences of the Greeks spread far beyond their borders, even when Persia remained the only superpower in the eastern Mediterranean.

What is significant is the role played by Greek culture in reinforcing a political program. Thus, Alexander the Great of the Macedonian nation would try to accommodate multiple communities in his empire. Yet his "attempt to unite the Greeks and the Persians into a new nation remained an unfulfilled dream. Alexander's successors insisted that they were, first of all, Macedonians and Greeks, and they made great efforts to promote and to maintain the Greek element in their countries."[47] The fact that Alexander's dream of an empire did not succeed does not mean that his program was a complete failure. He had instilled into the region a persistent sense of the importance of Greek culture for its heritage.

Modern historians, in describing a historical cultural phenomenon, have commonly used the term Hellenism; however, the term should be understood as an amalgamation of the Greeks and other original cultures. Hellenism is, thus, a "combination" or "amalgamation" of two or more cultures:

It is advisable, therefore, to use the term Hellenism primarily as a designation of the historical period which begins with Alexander the Great and ends with the final conquest of the east by the Romans, at which point the Roman imperial period began. The most characteristic phenomenon of the Hellenistic period is "Hellenization," namely, the expansion of the Greek language and culture and, most of all, the establishment of the Greeks' political dominion over other nations of the east. Never was there any question as to which element would predominate: even the successor states of the Hellenistic empires claimed to represent the Greek inheritance. Even when Greek culture encountered the Romans, the Greek element prevailed: the whole eastern part of the Roman Empire remained essentially Greek, and the Greek language and culture as well as Greek religion gained considerable ground even in the Latin west. Thus, Hellenism continued to be effective throughout the Roman imperial period, and insofar as the Roman Empire was Hellenized, it found its natural continuation in the Byzantine period. Indeed, Christianity, which had its beginnings in the early Roman imperial period, was rapidly Hellenized and appeared in the Roman world as a Hellenistic religion, specifically as the heir to an already Hellenized Jewish religion.[48]

A pattern of conquest is being described through cultural domination. In this sense, the Greeks "brought an advantage which no other conqueror before them possessed: a highly developed economy which could be immediately utilized to stimulate the economic growth of the new realms."[49] The Greeks became a conquered people, yet "the ruling class occupied all important positions in the administration and in the army."[50]

This pattern of cultural domination played out in the land of Israel as well, which, like other nations, was under the control and influence of Greek culture from the conquest by Alexander the Great onward into the Roman era. Because of the Hellenistic influence, scholars have commonly accepted Greek as the spoken language by many inhabitants of the region. Josephus, the historian, who met Poppaea, the wife of Nero, undoubtedly spoke with her in Greek. However, "the Greek-speaking population in the land was rather small, limited to government officials and clerks and some of the citizenry of Hellenistic cities."[51]

Clearly, the Jews of the major Diaspora were under the influence of Hellenistic Greek. Written communication between Israel and those in the Diaspora, Ptolemais, Scythopolis, Egypt, Syria, Asia Minor, Greece, and Italy, was in the Greek language. Yet those Jews residing in those Greek cities did not use Greek names; "rather, the ancient Semitic form such as Acco, Beth Shean, and Lod have remained in use down to the present century."[52] Modern Biblical scholars have also taught that during the reign of Trajan (117 C.E.), Aramaic (a Semitic language closely related to Hebrew) was the spoken language of Babylonian Jews. Aramaic inscriptions discovered from the Second Temple period confirmed an Aramaic influence. However, this influence should not be exaggerated:

> The role of Aramaic in every day life should not be exaggerated. Many scholars who admit the widespread use of Hebrew in the last few generations of the Second Temple period claim that Temple services were conducted in Aramaic. While there were a number of Aramaic words and phrases associated with the administration of the Temple and Temple area, the vast majority of references relating to Temple life reflect the use

of Hebrew there. The Mishnah preserves many descriptions of various aspects of every day life in the Temple, including statements of Temple officials which almost always are in Hebrew. Moreover, to date all of the inscriptions found in the Temple area are written in Hebrew, except for two Greek inscriptions, originally part of a balustrade surrounding the inner Temple, which warned Gentiles not to go beyond that point.[53]

The archeological evidence suggests that an additional, less obvious act of cultural polities was played out when the Christian Jews separated from the Jewish community. Christian scholars have fostered the idea that various Jewish communities expanded in the Roman Empire. The Jewish communities were faced with the problem of cultural assimilation, which the Romans practiced under what is called Hellenism. Indeed, their greatest concern was the loss of their identity as a people, which was their religion.[54]

Evidence of a further Semitic-speaking community is found in other sources such as Mishnaic Hebrew. Modern Christian Hellenistic scholars wrongly suggest that neither Hebrew nor Aramaic was part of the reading in synagogues. They go so far as even questioning the relationship between Hebrew and Aramaic in the land of Israel, even though evidence supports the fact that the Torah and Prophets, as well as prayers, were read in Hebrew. These same scholars have concluded somewhat falsely that, in the Judaic regions of the Middle East, Aramaic was the spoken language used in the market places and family circles.

In clear view of the evidence supporting a Hebrew-speaking people in the land of Israel, scholars "have persisted in claiming that this 'Hebrew was actually some type of Aramaic dialect then prevalent among the Jews of the land.'"[55] That is, the success of Hellenization and Hellenism in the Middle East and the Roman Empire has led scholars to assume it as a general principle.

The Dead Sea Scrolls and the documents of the Bar-Kokhba revolt (132-135 C.E.) conclusively settled the question concerning Mishnaic Hebrew, whether it was an artificial or a living language of the day. Without a doubt, these documents provided letters indicting Hebrew slang and abbreviated Hebrew forms as everyday speech. These discoveries prompted the Biblical scholar, J. T. Milik, to conclude the following:

> The thesis of such scholars as Segal, Ben-Yehuda and Klausner that Mishnaic Hebrew was a language spoken by the population of Judea in the Persian and Greco-Roman periods can no longer be considered as assumption, but rather an established fact. (*Discoveries in the Judaean Desert*, 2:70).[56]

During the twentieth century, between 1947 and 1963, scholars began to determine, "beyond dispute, that Hebrew was not merely in the exposition of Scripture and for prayer but also for non-religious purposes."[57] About six hundred manuscript fragments were found, and 179 are direct excerpts from the Old Testament. Ten documents unfold the organizational rules and conditions of the Essene sect very closely associated with Jesus. Critically, nine of the ten were written in Hebrew and only one in Aramaic. The evidence is clear, "Even the manuscript known as the copper scroll" and the fragments from the second century of the Christian era testify to the use of Hebrew at the time of the Roman occupation.[58]

The cultural landscape of Judaism and emerging Christianity thus lay far apart from that of Hellenized Rome, especially in its distinctions between a scholarly and a lay language. Thus, Rabbinic literature adhered to a distinct image of their own culture: "when the Jewish writers of the Second Temple period referred to Hebrew, they meant Hebrew and not Aramaic,"[59] During the period of the Sages, they also clearly differentiated between the Hebrew and Aramaic sections of the Bible. The Mishnah states, "The Aramaic passages in Ezra and Daniel render the hands unclean. If any of these passages were written in Hebrew, or if passages from the Hebrew Scriptures were written in Aramaic...they do not render the hands unclean" (Mishnah, *Yadayim* 4:5).[60]

Hebrew literacy was, therefore, the focus of attention as an assertion of group identity for the Jews. According to Safrai, Josephus writes in his introduction to *The Jewish Antiquities*, "for it [his book] will embrace our entire ancient history and political constitution, translated from the Hebrew records, (*Antiquities* 1:5)." The Hebrew records he refers to are the Bible.[61] The Jewish War of 66 also provides some evidence, according to Josephus, who delivered a message from Titus asking the inhabitants to surrender. Josephus approached the wall of Jerusalem, and, he desired not only John of Gischala to understand, he also desired the population to hear his message which for both he delivered in Hebrew. In 70 C.E., at the time of the destruction of the Temple, it is thus clear that the spoken language of Jerusalem was Hebrew and not Greek or Aramaic.

In some academic circles a position is held that a high percentage of the Galilean population was religiously uneducated, and thus knew and used less Hebrew. However, literary sources provide no indication that this claim is correct. True, in Rabbinic literature there are a number of "anti-Galilee" statements; these may well point to a status break within the community rather than to a questioning of the value of Hebrew literacy. The literature records, culturally and spiritually, Galilee may have been closer to Jerusalem than Judea:

There is a statement in rabbinic literature that the Judeans retained the teaching of their Torah scholars because they were careful in the use of their language, while the Galileans, who were not so careful with their speech, did not retain their learning (Babylonian Talmud, Eruvin 53a-b, Jerusalem Talmud, Berachot 4b *et al.*). While this saying is sometimes considered to be evidence for the dominance of Aramaic over Hebrew in the Galilee because some of the examples discussed are in Aramaic, it actually only refers to the Judeans' feeling that Galileans mispronounced the guttural letter *het* and *'ayin* and dropped the weak letters *alef* and *hey*. This in no way reflects on the cultural status of Galilee, nor does it show that the use of Hebrew was less common there than in Judea or Jerusalem.[62]

In the above statement it is clear that this provides evidence that points to a Jewish lifestyle in and during the Diaspora. The Gospels provided yet another excellent historical document which supports Hebrew as the spoken language of that day, a fact still not taught in Bible colleges and universities today. Evidence such as the "discovery of the Hebrew Ben Sira (Ecclesiasticus), of the Dead Sea Scrolls, and of the Bar Kokhba Letters, and in the light of more profound studies within the language of the Jewish Sages, it is accepted that most people were fluent in Hebrew."[63] Not only did Jesus speak Hebrew, according to Acts 21:40, *Paul stood on the stairs, and beckoned with the hand unto the people. And when there was made a great silence, he spoke unto them in the Hebrew tongue, saying.* This material thus suggests that there should be no ground for assuming that Greek or Aramaic was the spoken language of this period.[64]

Finally, shortly after the death of Jesus, a school of interpretation known as Gnosticism quickly gained influence in Christian teachings. A brief look at the Gnostic gospels and the influence Marcion had on the early Church is important to further understanding the Hellenistic influence on the Gospels. During this early stage of Christian history, the Greek word *gnosis* embraced all schools of religious and philosophical knowledge. Gnosticism grew out of several philosophical schools. These schools can be traced back to Simon Magus who was "dependent on Heraclitus, Valentine on Pythagoras and Plato, Basilides on Aristotle, Marcion on Empedocles."[65]

Philip Schaff, considered among Christian scholars as an authority on Church history, states, "Gnosticism, with its syncretistic tendency, is no isolated fact. It struck its roots deep in the mighty revolution of ideas induced by the fall of the old religions and the triumph of the new."[66] Most important for the present purposes: Gnosticism is closely associated with the Oriental approach, and Christianity followed a Grecian mode of Biblical interpretation. Thus, Gnosticism was also referenced with Judaism because it is characterized by a vigorous pursuit of learning. It is more than clear that the only major thing the Gnostics had in common with Judaism was their quest for intellectual learning through textual study. History has already established the heretic dogma of the Gnostic school. Marcion and his Marcionites (followers) were products of this Gnostic school. The history of the Gnostics and the teachings of Marcion are well documented. However, "the heresy of Marcion's teachings tainted unfavorably the progression of ecclesiastical doctrines. Christianity became defined as the antithesis of the faith experience of the Jewish people. The acknowledgment of roots, relatedness and interconnectedness between the mother, Judaism, and her daughter faith was obscured by a battle of hate and polemic."[67] Thus the establishment of a philosophical movement that joined in the religious discussions of this age helped to further the choice of Hellenism over Judaism.

NOTES FOR CHAPTER 2

[45] Koester, pp. xix, xxx: "The cities emancipated themselves from local and ethic peculiarities and became centers of the most important economic, cultural, and religious activities, yet they had to solve questions of morality and religion that emerged from worldwide political, economic and social problems. It is exactly these major Hellenistic cities in which early Christianity was formed and developed its potential as a new world religion. A historically-oriented Introduction to the New Testament thus must begin with a consideration of the Hellenistic age in order to clarify the presupposition for the formation and expansion of early Christianity." Pp. 1-2.

[46] Koester, p. 2: "The victory of the Greeks over the Persians deeply impressed itself upon the Greek mind. This theme found manifold expression in Greek literature, in poetry and fiction as well as in political and scientific writings, and led to reflections about the fundamental differences

to come. The Greeks had successfully withstood the onslaught of an eastern superpower. The consciousness of the superiority of Greek education, Greek culture, and of the Greek gods formed not only the Greek mind, but also that of other nations, later including even the Romans, although they were to become the master of the Greeks."

[47]Koester, p. 39.

[48]Koester, pp. 39-40.

[49]Koester, p. 41: "The Greek language and Greek methods of education dominated culturally, but the centers of education shifted to Alexandria, Pergamum, and Rhodes. The non-Greek contribution was present from the beginning, but was not always immediately recognizable, since it made its appearance by means of the Greek language and Greek forms and structures of organization."

[50]Koester, p. 40.

[51]Shmuel Safrai, *Spoken Languages in the Time of Jesus*, (Jerusalem: Jerusalem Perspective) pp. 1-2: "The official Greek names of such cities as Ptolemais, Scythopolis or Diospolis were not maintained by their residents."

[52]Safrai, p. 2: "The average resident of such cities most likely referred to them by their Semitic names."

[53]Safrai, p. 3.

[54]Avi-Yonah, p. 72: "Opposition to Greek culture was therefore strongest among the popular preacher or Haggadistis, who were mainstay of the zealot party. In their eyes knowledge of Greek was the first step to perdition, to the complete assimilation of Israel amongst the nations. They pointed to the fact that most of the known apostates had begun their career of betrayal by meeting Gentiles and reading their books, especially the works of the Greek philosophers. The saying was current in these circles."

[55]Safrai, p. 4: "It has even been claimed that the Hebrew in which the Mishnah was written was an artificial Language of the Midrash, (house of study), which was translation from Aramaic, or at the very least heavily influenced by Aramaic. However, some seventy years ago a number of Jewish scholars in Palestine (later the State of Israel) began to see that the Hebrew of the Mishnah had been a living and vibrant language, spoken in the house of study, synagogue, on the street and at home. Mishnaic Hebrew does not deal only with matters of religion, but mentions, for instance, the names of dozens of implements used at the time, and records thousands of events and sayings about mundane, secular aspects of life."

[56]Safrai, p. 5: "Samaritan commentaries and translations of the Scriptures have preserved traces of Mishnaic Hebrew. The language of Christians in the land of Israel, particularly those living in the southern part of the land, also shows the impact of Mishnaic Hebrew. These Christians continued to write in Aramaic until at least the sixth century, and their Aramaic was greatly influenced by Mishnaic Hebrew, but not at all by Biblical Hebrew."

[57]Risto Santala, *The Messiah in The New Testament in The Light of Rabbinical Writings* (Jerusalem: Keren Ahvah Meshihit, 1984) p. 44.

[58]Santala, p. 45: "Professor Frank Cross, considered one of the foremost authorities on these manuscripts, made a comparative study of the copyists' linguistic proficiency and found that their grammatical and syntactic competence in Aramaic was clearly inferior to their performance in Hebrew."

[59]Safrai, p. 5: "They did not confuse the two languages, but distinguished quite clearly between Hebrew and Aramaic, referring to the latter either as Aramaic, targun or; Syriac' (sursit)."

[60]Safrai, pp. 5-6.

[61]Safrai, p. 6: "In his discussion of creation and the Sabbath he states: For which reason we also pass this day in repose from toil and call it Sabbath, a word which in the Hebrew language means 'rest' (Antiquities 1:33). This makes sense only if Hebrew and not Aramaic is intended because in Aramaic the root n-u-h rather than sh-b-t, is used for to rest."

[62]Safrai, p. 8.

[63]Flusser, p. 11: "The spoken languages among the Jews of that period were Hebrew, Aramaic, and to an extent Greek. Until recently, it was believed by numerous scholars that the language spoken by Jesus' disciples was Aramaic. It is possible that Jesus did, from time to time, make use of the Aramaic language. But during that period Hebrew was both the daily language and the language of study. The Gospel of Mark contains a few Aramaic words, and this was what misled scholars."

[64]Flusser, p. 11: "This question of the spoken language is especially important for understanding the doctrines of Jesus. There are sayings of Jesus which can be rendered both into Hebrew and Aramaic; but there are some which can only be rendered into Hebrew, and none of them can be rendered only into Aramaic. One can thus demonstrate the Hebrew origins of the Gospels by retranslating them into Hebrew. It appears that the earliest documents concerning Jesus were written works, taken down by his disciples after his death. Their language was early Rabbinic Hebrew with strong undercurrents of Biblical Hebrew. Even in books of the New Testament which were originally composed in Greek, such as the Pauline Epistles, there are clear traces of the Hebrew language: and the terminology in those books of the New Testament which were composed in Greek is often intelligible only when we know the original Hebrew terms."

[65]Schaff, p. 446: "Of all these systems Platonism had the greatest influence, especially on the Alexandrian Gnostics; though not so much in its original Hellenic form, as in its later orientalzed eclectic and mystic cast, of which Neo-Platonism was another fruit."

[66]Schaff, p. 447: "Gnosticism has accordingly been regarded as more or less parallel with the heretical form of Judaism, with Essenism, Theorapentism, Philo's philosophico-religious system, and with the Cabbala, the origin of which probably dates as far back as the first century."

[67]Young, p. 24: "The anti-Judaism of the church has roots running deep into the core of her history. The early-second-century heretic Marcion completely rejected the Hebrew Bible. Although many church leaders fought his doctrines, at times Marcion's theology managed to infiltrate orthodox teachings As Christians, we have learned about Judaism from one-sided accounts of inner struggles within the church and have viewed Jews and Judaism from our own perspective. We receive a derivative view of Judaism based upon false evidence. Without having read the ancient literature Israel's left behind, we malign Judaism as a religious system of legalism with a salvation-by-works infrastructure."

CHAPTER 3

THE KINGDOM OF HEAVEN IN ITS HISTORICAL

SETTING

The historical documents of the Gospels Matthew, Mark, and Luke are entirely Hebraic. These synoptic Gospels provide us with key elements in their original setting, which establish without argument a Semitic foundation. One such concept is the phrase "The Kingdom of Heaven," which in Hebrew has a distinct meaning and purpose beyond what we had previously understood. The Hebraism which is beneath this concept did not originate in the Synoptic Gospels; it is a part of deep Hebraic roots that the heretic Marcion and others called the "Old Testament."

The Invisible Kingdom

Solomon Schechter, in *Aspects of Rabbinic Theology: Major Concepts of The Talmud*, states: "the term Kingdom of Heaven must therefore be taken in the sense in which heaven is equivalent to God, not locally, as if the kingdom were located in the celestial spheres."[68] The evidence used by the rabbis to establish that there is a Kingdom of Heaven was that kingdom existed in the lives of the people of Israel (Deut. 6:4). Today, that same declaration of God's kingship can be seen in the prayer *Malchut*,[69] which states:

> The foremost among these are the concluding lines of the kingship benediction recited on the New Year, running thus: "Our God and God of our fathers, reign thou in thy glory over the whole universe, and be exalted above all the earth in thine honour, and shine forth in the splendor and excellence of thy might, upon all the inhabitants of thy world, that whatsoever hath been made may know that thou hast made it, and whatsoever hath breath in its nostrils, may say, the Lord God of Israel is King, and his dominion ruleth over all...O purify our hearts to serve thee in truth, for thou art God in truth, and thy word is truth, and endureth forever. Blessed art thou O Lord, King over all the earth, who sanctifies Israel and the Day of Memorial."[70]

Exodus 15:18 supports the position of the rabbis that God's kingship is an everlasting kingdom. The text says: *The Lord shall reign for ever and ever.* On Midrash Rabbah 23:13, one finds the phrase: *so that they will not be prideful and know that the kingdom of Heaven* (Malchut Shamayim) *is over them.*

In Exodus Rabbah 23:13, the text gives an excellent example of how the phrase "The Kingdom of Heaven" establishes a highly exalted domain where God is King and how other subjects are within this domain. The text reads as follows:

> I will bring unto The Lord, for He is Highly Exalted. It is written, *Deck thyself now with majesty and*

excellency (Job XI, 10). All things exalt themselves over something else; darkness exalts over the deep, because it is above it, and the wind exalts itself over the water because it is above it; fire exalts itself above the wind because it is above it, and the heavens exalt themselves over the fire, because they are above it, but God is exalted over everything – hence: For He is Highly Exalted. R. Abin said: Four kinds of exalted beings have been created in the world. The most exalted of all living creatures is man; of birds, the eagle; of cattle, the ox; and of wild beasts, the lion. All of these received royalty and had greatness bestowed upon them, and they are set under the chariot of God, as it says, *as for the likeness of their faces, they had the face of a man; and they four had the face of a lion...and... also the face of an eagle* (Ezek. 1, 10). Why was this? So that they should not exalt themselves in the world and they should know that the Kingdom of Heaven is over them. For this reason does it says, *For one higher than the high watcheth, and there, are higher than they.*[71]

It is clear a declaration of kingship is bestowed in the above statement and how God becomes king over this Kingdom of Heaven.

In Psalms 99:1-5, we see another picture of God as king. The Psalmist records the following:

The Lord reigns, let the nations tremble; he sits enthroned between the cherubim, let earth shake. Great is the Lord in Zion; he is exalted over all the nations. Let them praise your great and awesome name – he is Holy. The King is mighty, he loves justice – you have established equity; in Jacob you have done what is just and right. Exalt the Lord our God and worship at his footstool; he is holy.

The parallel text found in Midrash on Psalms, interprets Psalms 99:1 as following:

The Lord reigneth; let the peoples tremble. R. Judah said in the name of R. Samuel: As long as the children of Israel are in exile, the kingdom of heaven is not at peace; yet the nations of the earth dwell unperturbed. When the children of Israel are redeemed, however, the kingdom of heaven will be at peace, but the peoples of the earth will tremble. Hence The Lord reigneth; let the peoples tremble. He is enthroned upon the cherubim; let the earth stagger – stagger this way and that way. Why? Because The Lord is great in Zion; and He is high above all the peoples. R. Johanan took the words The Lord is great in Zion to mean that God is great because of what He has done to Zion. His own house He has not spared; therefore, when He returns to punish the destroyers thereof, how much great in Zion as follows: When the Lord causes His presence to return to Zion, then will He be great in Zion. R. Johanan said: A verse in Scripture supports R. Hanina; When the Lord shall build up Zion, then He shall appear in His glory (Ps. 102:17).[72]

In Rabbinic sources the concept "Kingdom of Heaven" refers to a kingdom that is in this world. An example of this point can be found in the Jewish Prayer Book where the prayer begins with על כן נקוה. Schechter points out the phrase על כן נקוה refers to the term מלכות דשי *the kingdom of the Almighty*, and may be safely regarded as a synonym for the term *Malchut Shamayim* (Kingdom of Heaven).[73] Thus, it is also safe to conclude that the phrase "Kingdom of the Almighty" can be translated as "Kingdom of Heaven" and refers to a kingdom established on earth by man's awareness that God is near to him. According to Schechter, "this is done, say the Rabbis, to the end that we may receive upon ourselves first the yoke of the kingdom and afterwards the yoke of the commandments."[74]

Kingdom of Heaven in Rabbinic Literature: The Kingdom and the Shema

In Rabbinic thought, the concept of receiving the yoke of the kingdom is an imperative to understanding the meaning of *Malkhut Shamaiym*. The expression to *receive upon himself the yoke of the kingdom of heaven*, is mainly spiritual.[75] It encompasses the attitude and character of the individual who declares God as King in all four corners of the world. The Gemara, a commentary within the Talmud, teaches that when reciting the *Shema*, "precepts must be performed with intent."[76] The Rabbis taught that the recitation of the *Shema: Hear, O Israel, the Lord our God, the Lord is one*,[77] should be done with *Kavanah* in mind.

These references were familiar to most Jews of that era. The Rabbis taught, during the Second Temple period while the Temple was still in operation, the *Shema* was recited twice daily; the recitation by the individual affirmed he or she had received the kingship of God or *Malkhut Shamayim* (Kingdom of Heaven). In Jubilees 12:19, a parallel is made by Abraham concerning the Oneness of God in the (*Shema*) and the Kingdom of God as (*Malkhut Shamayim*). The text reads:

And he [Abram] prayed on that night, saying: My God, the Most High God, You alone are God to me...And you and your kingdom I have chosen.[78]

Abram's acknowledgment of God as his only God was based upon the recital of the *Shema*, according to the Rabbis. It was Abram, the friend of God, who was "the first to call God master *'Adoni*,' a name which declares God to be the ruler of the world, and concerned with the actions of men."[79]

Moreover, the Rabbis taught that, with Abraham, the kingship of God returned. For through him righteousness and justice, the two ruling principles that are the very foundation of God's throne (Psa. 89:14), were enthroned. In Genesis 24:3, Abraham's acknowledgment of God, "I will make thee swear by the Lord, the God of heaven, and the God of the earth," is equal to Deuteronomy 6:4, "Hear, O Israel: The Lord our God is one Lord." The Rabbis taught that, when one recites the *Shema*, that person is affirming, as Abraham did, that He (God) is the one and only God. In consequence, this action of reciting the *Shema* is also a declaration of choosing to take upon oneself the "Kingdom of Heaven." Another important text supporting the above connections is found in Jubilees 12:19. It also parallels with *Berakhoth* 2:2 and supports the position that a recital of the *Shema* is the same as accepting the yoke of God's kingdom. The text states:

> R. Joshua b. Karha said; Why does the section, "Hear, O Israel" (Deuteronomy 6:4-9), precede "And it shall come to pass, if you shall hearken" (Deuteronomy 11:13-21)? So that a man shall first receive upon himself the yoke of the commandments.[80]

The "yoke" and the "Kingdom" exist in a very specific relationship to each other, a relationship fully echoed in the *Shema*. The Rabbis divided the *Shema* into two sections: the first established God's kingship by each individual accepting the yoke of the Kingdom of Heaven; the second establishes the yoke of the commandments of God. R. Joshua b. Karha distinguishes the yoke of the Kingdom of Heaven from that of the yoke of the commandments. Schechter explained that "the law [the yoke of the commandments] is thus only a necessary consequence of the kingdom [the yoke of the kingdom], but not identical with it."[81] In Midrash Exodus 20:11, the text unfolds the distinction between the yoke of the Kingdom of Heaven and the yoke of the commandments of God. The text reads:

Thou Shalt Not Have Other Gods Before Me. Why is this said? Because it says: "I am the Lord Thy God."

Likewise, God said to Israel: "I am the Lord Thy God, thou shalt not have other gods – I am He whose reign you have taken upon yourselves in Egypt." And when they said to Him: "Yes, yes," He continued: "Now, just as you accepted My reign [which is the same as saying just as you accepted the yoke of My kingship], you must also accept My decrees [that is the yoke of my commandments]: Thou shalt not have other gods before Me."[82]

In another example, the text asked the following question:

Why were the Ten Commandments not said at the beginning of the Torah? They give a parable. To what may this be compared? To the following: a king who entered a province said to the people: May I be your King? But the people said to him: Have you done anything good for us that you should rule over us? What did he do then? He built the city wall for them, he brought in the water supply for them, and he fought their battles. Then when he said to them: May I be your king? Then He said to them: I am to be your King. And they said to Him: Yes, yes. For when they all stood before Mount Sinai to receive the Torah they all made up their mind alike to accept the reign of God joyfully. Furthermore, they pledged themselves for one another.[83]

Again, it is clear that the yoke of the Kingdom of Heaven does not automatically mean the yoke of His laws, God's rule [kingship] over every Israelite. Instead, the Rabbis taught that God himself must first be accepted as King if His decrees are to be carried out in the heart of His people. This is why the first section of the *Shema*, Hear O Israel our God the Lord is One, is equated with the Kingship of God; while "the acceptance of the yoke of the kingdom of heaven means to acknowledge the God who is One and Unique, and to bear witness that there is no other god."[84]

This theological point is echoed elsewhere. In *Berachoth* 13b, the text records, "Once you have declared Him King over [all that is] above and below and over the four quarters of the heaven, no more is required."[85] Also in *Berachoth* 13b, it states:

Our Rabbis taught: *Hear, O Israel, the Lord our God, the Lord is One*: this was R. Judah the Prince's recital of the *Shema*. Rab said once to R. Hiyya: I do not see Rabbi accept upon himself the yoke of the kingdom of heaven. He replied to him: Son of Princes! In the moment when he passes his hand over his eyes, he accepts upon himself the yoke of the kingdom of heaven. Does he finish it afterwards or does he not finish it afterwards? Bar Kappara said: He does not finish it afterwards; R. Simeon son of Rabbi said, he does finish it afterwards. Said Bar Kappara to R. Simeon the son of Rabbi: On my view that he does not finish it afterwards, there is a good reason why Rabbi always is anxious to take a lesson in which there is mention of the exodus from Egypt. But on your view that he does finish it afterwards, why is he anxious to take such a lesson? So as to mention the going forth from Egypt at the proper time.[86]

In the above text, the acceptance of the invisible aspect of God's Kingdom is expressed by an unconditional surrendering of the mind and heart to God's will. Thus Israel, His subject, surrenders its free will, thereby exemplifying what it means to receive the yoke of God's Kingdom.

In Deuteronomy 4:39, the text reads as follows: "Know therefore this day, and consider it in thine heart, that the Lord he is God in heaven above, and upon the earth beneath: there is none else." The Rabbis refer to passages such as this and others to show the reasons God's subjects declared their invisible trust in His kingship. Schechter wrote that the yoke of the commandments is consequential upon the acceptance of the Kingdom of Heaven. Therefore, the technical terms relating to the *Shema* represent the one who receives upon himself the Kingdom of Heaven and the one who receives upon himself the yoke of the Kingdom of Heaven.

God Received As King

The Rabbis interpreted Torah concerning the Kingdom of Heaven as instructing Israel in the following:

Receive upon yourselves the yoke of the Kingdom of Heaven, and judge one another in the fear of God; and conduct yourselves towards each other in loving kindness.[87]

Urbach reinforces the above statement by writing:

The purpose of the Torah and the precepts is the acceptance of the yoke of the kingdom of heaven, which finds expression in the fear [i.e., reverence] and love of the Lord. But even when explaining the order of the Ten Commandments on Mount Sinai, and likewise the order of the sections of the *Shema'* the Tannaim ruled that the intended and desired procedure for a Jew is first to assume the yoke of the Kingdom of Heaven and then the yoke of the commandments.[88]

Also in the Midrash on I Samuel 8:7, Rabbi Simeon B. Yohai clearly equates the term *Malchut Shamayim* with the personage of God. The context establishes our link. The elders of Israel demanded that Samuel appoint a king over them like the other nations. God spoke unto Samuel saying:

Hearken (listen as in, be obedient) unto the voice of the people in all that they say unto you,

For they have rejected Me, refused that I should be King over them.

Rabbi Simeon B. Yohai, taught that God told Samuel the following:

Surely three things they [the Israelites] will reject: The Kingdom of Heaven, אותי the kingship of The house of David, and the building of the Temple. They have rejected all three in the days of Rehoboam.[89]

Rabbi Simeon B. Yohai undoubtedly equated, (אותי) [Me] of I Samuel 8:7 with *Malkhut Shamayim*. Hence, to reject God is to cast off the yoke of the Kingship of Heaven. It is a denial of God. In another example of the uses of the transition to *yoke*, Rabbi Yohanan B. Zakki was asked by his disciples:

> Why of all the parts of the body is it the ear of [the Hebrew] slave that had to be pierced [as the mark of his being a bond servant], He answered the ear, which heard on Mount Sinai: *There shall not be to you any other gods before Me* (Exo. 20:1), and broke from upon himself the yoke of the Kingdom of Heaven and received upon himself the yoke of the human being, the ear that heard before Mount Sinai: For unto Me the *children of Israel are servants* and this man went and received another master. Therefore, let his ear be pierced through because he observed not that which his ear had heard.[90]

In this explanation, those who accept the yoke of the Kingdom of Heaven become servants of "the King of the gods and Master of all dominion."[91] The Mishnah provides another example of our readings; it states:

> Be not like that minister to the Master for the sake of receiving a bounty, but be like slaves that minister to the master not for the sake of receiving a bounty, and let the fear of Heaven be upon you.[92]

The proclamation made to Israel to serve God is not a call to the state of bondage in which slaves are to a tyrant, but to be like servants who serve with love, as stated in Exodus 34:6,7.

I Am The Lord

Another important phrase the Rabbis deduced from Scriptures is a technical expression for affirming the Kingship of God (עול מלכות שמים רם מלכות שמים) *yoke of the commandments raises the Kingdom of Heaven.* The above phrase is used by the Rabbis to express the phrase taken from Exodus 20:2, *I am the Lord thy God...*and Exodus 20:1-3. These passages are significant for understanding how the Rabbis arrived at their interpretation of the Kingship of God as it refers to *Malkhut Shamayim.* They based their understanding of God's Kingship in these passages where it was covered. However, it is also important to note that the first section of the *Shema, Hear O Israel, the Lord our God the Lord is One,* is another phrase used by the Rabbis to express God's Kingship or the Kingdom of Heaven. According to the Rabbis the above phrase is also found in Exodus 20:1-3 which provides a parallel account of the exclusiveness of God. The text says:

> And God spoke all these words, saying: I am the Lord thy God, who brought you out of the land of Egypt, out of the house of bondage. Thou shalt have no other gods before Me.

In both the *Shema* and *I am the Lord your God*, the central figure is the Lord God Himself. He alone is to be affirmed as the King of all creation. He is:

> King from one end of the world to the other, and the entire world – every part of it – is His, as is said, *Behold, unto the Lord thy God belonged the heaven, and the heaven of heavens, the earth with all that therein is* (Deut. 10:14).[93]

The Rabbis taught that when God declared *I am the Lord thy God*, he was stating:

> I am He who was in Egypt and I am He who was at the sea. I am He who was at Sinai, I am He

who was in the past and I am He who will be in the future. I am He who is in this world and I am He who will be in the world to come, as it is said: See now that I, even I, am He, (Deut. 32:39). And it says Even to old age I am the same (Isa. 46:4). And it says: Thus said the Lord, the king of Israel, and his redeemer the Lord of Hosts. I am the first, and I am the last (ibid. 44:6).[94]

Rabbi Simon B. Johai made the equation of the Kingship of God with "I am the Lord your God" as the following:

I am the Lord your God (Lev. 18:2) means: I am He whose reign you have taken upon yourselves at Sinai, and when they said: Yes, yes, He continued: Well, you have accepted My reign, now accept My decrees: after the doings of the land of Egypt, etc. (ibid. v. 3). What is said here: I am the Lord thy God who brought thee out from the land of Egypt, means: I am He whose reign you have taken upon yourselves, and when they said to Him. Yes, yes, He continued: You have accepted My reign, now accept My decrees: Thou shalt not have other gods.[95]

Rabbi Nathan affirms that the kingship is declared by אני הי [I am the Lord], which is derived from one of the kingship verses [Numbers 10:10]...I am the Lord your God. He wrote:

I am the Lord your God. This is the kingship, if so why did the sages choose to place the kingship first and afterwards the remembrance, and the shofar? [they said], First proclaim God King and then pray to Him for mercy in order to be remembered by Him.[96]

The phrases *I am the Lord your God* and *Hear O Israel the Lord our God* are similar but not exact in form. However, they are both identical in content in that they affirm the unity of God and the kingship of His rule and reign.

The textual evidence suggests that these citations had real correlations. That is, they were not simply proverbs but guides to action. For instance, Israel acknowledged this great respect and reverence when they received the yoke of the commandments. Thereby, "said the Community of Israel: The Holy One, blessed be He,...gave me banners of Torah, and precepts and good deeds, and in great love I accepted them (Cant. 2:4)"[97] Though the yoke of the Kingdom of Heaven was consequent upon the yoke of the commandments, the Rabbis attributed a significant role to the receiving of the Torah. According to Rabbinic interpretation, God said, *I am the Lord who brought you out of the land of Egypt.* Jacob Neusner, quoting from Sifre *On Deuteronomy* (Piska 163) writes:

> It was on this stipulation that I brought you up out of the land of Egypt, on the condition that you accept on yourselves the yoke of the religious duties. For whoever accepts the yoke of the religious duties also affirms the exodus from Egypt, but whoever rejects the yoke of the commandments rejects the exodus from Egypt.[98]

Neusner points out that the Exodus event was a type of accepting the rule and reign of God, which parallels accepting the yoke of the Kingdom of Heaven, the yoke of the commandments, and the yoke of Torah.

The above example proves the concept "Kingdom of Heaven" clearly existed before it appears in the Gospels. The references found in the Hebrew Scriptures, in late and early Rabbinic sources, place the concept in its natural historical roots. In light of such overwhelming historical material, what is puzzling is why the early Church Fathers chose to overlook these historical roots. Thus accordingly, The "Kingdom of Heaven" example proves ample evidence that many elements played an important role in establishing Hellenistic thought as the foundation of Christianity. In the next chapter, comparing and contrasting the Hellenized text with a Hebraic interpretation of Matthew chapter 5 will provide a look at these passages of text. Also a closer look will be taken at New Testament Christian scholars and their commentaries, which provides biblical interpretations on the book of the Gospels. These examinations will reveal how much the Hellenistic culture has influenced how the text is read today.

NOTES FOR CHAPTER 3

[68]Schechter, *Aspects of Rabbinic Theology: Major Concepts of the Talmud.* (New York: Schocken Books, 1909) p. 89.

[69]A. Buchler, *Types of Jewish-Palestinian Piety: The Ancient Pious Men.* (New York: KTAV Publishing House, Inc. 1968) pp. 41-42.

[70]Schechter, *Aspects of Rabbinic Theology*, pp. 93-94.

[71]Rabbi Dr. S.M. Lehrman, *Midrash Rabbah, Exodus* (London, New York: The Soncino Press 1983) p. 291.

[72]Midrash of Psalms 99:1.

[73]Schechter, *Aspects of Rabbinic Theology*, p. 89.

[74]Schechter, *Aspects of Rabbinic Theology*, p. 91.

[75]Hertz, *The Authorized Daily Prayer Book with a New Translation* (London, 1890) p. 112: "The yoke of the kingdom of heaven, Kingdom, here means kingship, and Heaven, is merely a synonym for God. To take upon oneself the yoke of the Kingdom of Heaven means, to recognize the rule of God in the heart and life of man. As to Yoke, it is well to remember that a yoke is

not imposed upon animals in order to torture them. To cause them to work without a yoke, that would be torture – and the field would remain unfilled. A yoke enables the animals to pull together in preparing the ground for human benefit. In the same way, when men in harmony and love take upon themselves the yoke of the kingdom of heaven, they resolve to pull together – to labour with their fellowmen for the furtherance of God's reign." 112.

[76]Rabbi Dr. I. Epstein, *The Babylonian Talmud Seder Zera'im* (London: The Soncino Press, 1958) p. 76.

[77]Max Kadushin, *The Rabbinic Mind* (New York: Bloch Publishing Company 1972) pp. 130-131: "The recital of "Hear, O Israel, the Lord is our God, the Lord is One" (Deut. 6:4) is the affirmation of Malkhut shamayim. This is emphasized by an insertion the Rabbis made between Deut. 6:4 and ibid., v. 5, the insertion reading:... It is of course inserted only in the liturgy, not in the text of the Bible. So habitually was this Ha-Shanah even though it does not contain any form of the root mlk, and thus the ten required "sovereignty" verses are completed. The martyrdom of R. Akita, connected with this declaration, is given richer background by Lieberman. The hour for the recital of the Shema had arrived just before his execution which was to have been by the sword; the declaration by Akiba of Malkut Shamayim, a declaration prohibited by decree because of its negation of emperor worship, caused the method of execution to be changed."

[78]H. F. D. Sparks, *Introduction to the Talmud and Midrash* (New York: Temple, 1931) p. 48.

[79]Solomon Schechter, *Aspects of Rabbinic Theology*, p. 84, Tama Debe Eliyyahu, Pirke R. Eliezer, p. 522: "This source states that when Abraham was born, he made known the name of the Holy One and proclaimed the

king of Sodom: I have lifted my hand unto the Lord God Most High, Possessor of heaven and earth (Gen. 14, 22) Thereupon in joy the Holy One Kissed both His hands, saying: Up to this moment on man <in My world> has called Me Lord and Most High, but <now in My world I have been called Lord and Most High>, for Abraham has just said, I have lifted my hand unto the Lord God Most High. Possessor of heaven and earth."

[80] Herbert Danby, ed., *The Mishnah: Seder Zeraim Berachoth* (New York: Oxford, 1933) p. 3.

[81] Schechter, *Aspects of Rabbinic Theology*, p. 91: "In this connection reference may be held to the following Midrashic passage alluding to Zech. 9:9 'Rejoice greatly, O daughter of Zion,...behold thy King is coming unto thee...God says to Israel:' 'Ye righteous of the world, the words of the Torah are important for me; ye were attached to the Torah, but did not hope for my kingdom. I take an oath that with regard to those who hope for my kingdom I shall myself bear witness for their claim merit for themselves'" (91).

[82] Jacob Z. Lauterbach, *Mekilta De – Rabbi Ishmael* vol. 2. (Philadelphia: The Jewish Publication Society of America, 1933) p. 238: "R. Simon b. Johai says: What is said further on: 'I am the Lord your God' (Lev. 18:2) means: 'I am He whose reign you have taken upon yourselves at Sinai,' and when they said: 'Yes, yes,' He continued: 'Well, you have accepted My reign, now accept My decrees'" (p. 238).

[83] Lauterbach, pp. 229-230.

[84] Ephraim E. Urbach, *The Sages: Their Concepts and Beliefs* (Cambridge MA: Harvard University Press, 1987) p. 400.

[85] Epstein, p. 78.

[86] Epstein, p. 79.

[87] L. Finkelstein, *Sifre Devarim* (New York: Jewish Theological Seminary, 1960) p. 323.

[88]Urbach, p. 400.

[89]A. Shinan, ed., *Midrash Shmuel* (Jerusalem: Hillel Press, 1984) pp. 13, 4, 42c.

[90]Talmud Jerusalem, Krotoshin Edition (Jerusalem: Hillel Press, 1982) p. 59d, 31.

[91]Metzger, p. 98.

[92]Danby, *Mishnah Aboth* 1,3, p. 446.

[93]Tanna Debe Elyyahu, *Eliyyahu Zuta* (Philadelphia: Jewish Publication Society, 1975) p. 410.

[94]Lauterbach, Vol. 2, pp. 231-232.

[95]Lauterbach, Vol. 2, p. 238.

[96]H. S. Horovitz, ed. *Sifra Al Bemidbar Vesifre Zuta* (Jerusalem: Wahramaan, 1966) p. 19b.

[97]Song of Songs Rabbath, p. 9: 103.

[98]Jacob Neusner, trans: *Sifra: An Analytical Translation*, Vols III (Atlanta. Scholars Press, 1988) pp. 2:227-228.

CHAPTER 4

MATTHEW'S REDACTOR

In the tradition of most New Testament scholars, the Gospel of Mark is considered to be the first of the gospels. This claim is based upon the two-document hypothesis, which states that Matthew and Luke draw their text from Mark's text. Today, a strong scholarly consensus remains among many NT scholars who continue to support the Marcan priority. Thus continuing the tradition of earlier German scholars who embraced the Marcan priority as a part of their hermeneutical methodology.[99] This theory is based upon the most probable sequential arrangement in the triple tradition of these Gospels. The scholarship of Karl Lachmann suggested that Matthew and Luke's gospels had a high level of agreement with Mark's gospel. However, neither the gospel of Matthew nor Luke agrees with each other as much as each agrees with Mark independently. Thus Lachmann suggests that Matthew and Luke depended on Mark's gospel in writing their basic outline.

In the text, *The Origins of the Gospel According to St. Matthew*, G. D. Kilpatrick set out to establish factors related to general indications of dates, places, and authorship. Accordingly, it is "derived from a consideration of the earliest traditions about the book, from the evidence for its use, from established conclusions about its sources, and from internal inferences implied by these conclusions."[100] Kilpatrick is working with the documentary hypothesis and the theory or position that "our Gospel is not by Matthew the Apostle. It depends on two or, more probably, three written sources, generally referred to as Mark, Q, and M, and in the handling of these sources it shows the features of a later period."[101] In defending his position Kilpatrick argues that:

> It is incredible that an Apostle should, for the greater part of his material, depend on written sources and, where he revises them, betray the outlook of a later period. These difficulties force us back to our alternative that by τα λογια Papias meant some document other than our Gospel. Two main suggestions have been made. The first is that by τα λογια Papias meant the document Q. On this hypothesis Q was originally written in Aramaic, and later a number of Greek translations of it were made, one of them being used in both our Matthew and Luke. But, if there were several translations of Q, how is it that Matthew and Luke independently used the same one, while of the others there is no sign? Again, it is not surprising that an anonymous document incorporated in both Matthew and Luke should later disappear, but it is surprising that a document, accepted as the work of the Apostle and in sufficiently widespread circulation in the latter part of the first century

to be used by these two evangelists, should have disappeared without a trace.[102]

Kilpatrick makes several points in the above statement that are important for our argument. First, he believes that "Papias," (a non-biblical source) referred to the document Q, and Q may be one of the possible writers of our text Matthew. Second he asserts that the Q hypothesis means that the text was first written in Aramaic and that later Greek translations were composed out of it.

While this age-old argument continues to this day, the solution may be as important as the discussion. Brad Young states: "The synoptic problem is not to prove beyond doubt that one approach is superior to all others. Rather it is urgent to recognize that Matthew and Luke can sometimes preserve texts that are more original than Mark."[103] As Young summarizes the Hebraic approach taken by many biblical scholars of today, he writes:

The approach presupposed or adopted as a working hypothesis in the work at hand is based to a large degree on the method developed by Lindsey and Flusser in Jerusalem. The Jerusalem school's approach accounts for the accumulated evidence that has resulted from the carefully studied in order to discover their sources. The attempt to rediscover what precious little can be known about the earthly Jesus involves the return to and the recovery of the early Greek sources for the life and teachings of Jesus and when possible to reconstruct them into Hebrew.[104]

Young established a crucial point that Hebrew sources need to come into play more directly when discussing the Biblical texts.

Robert L. Lindsey, in *A Hebrew Translation of the Gospel of Mark*, strongly argues, in opposition to Kilpatrick, that the Marcan redaction of the Greek Gospels is an extensive series of excellent Hebraic-Greek narratives and sayings in context. Lindsey discovered that the Greek Gospel of Luke translates back into Hebrew word for word, thus persevering and revealing a Hebrew text in "Greek dress."[105] An illustration can be seen in the following:

Luke 22, 67-70

Art thou the Christ? Tell us. And he said unto them. If I tell you, ye will not believe: And if I also ask you, ye will not answer me, nor let me go. Hereafter shall the Son of man sit on the right hand of the power of God. Then said they all, Art thou then the Son of God? And he said unto them, Ye say that I am.

The above passage unfolds yet another important part of the puzzle in illuminating clear interpretations of Jesus' teachings. He employed an aspect of His cultural language that goes beyond just vocabulary and syntax analogies used by Kilpatrick. As reported in such textual passages, Lindsey used a style of textual evaluation which Hellenistic scholars knew nothing about, thereby hindering their ability to translate the Gospels accurately. Because of the groundbreaking work by Lindsey, scholars and students who are fluent in Hebrew and Greek are now translating the gospels with clarity of understanding never achieved before. Lindsey demonstrates the specific forms of Hebraism found in the above text in Luke by stating the following:

However, the Synoptic patterns and rabbinic sophistication of the passage is fully as remarkable. As in all of Luke it is not Jesus who uses the word

Messiah about himself, this word is employed by the chief priests who are trying to get Jesus to "level" with them and confess the thing his actions and speech have long hinted at but not made explicit. Faced with hostile interrogators who are nevertheless conscious of their duty to get the facts Jesus does "level" with them by pointedly telling them that he cannot expect them to believe the truth if he says it and that he cannot even "ask" them anything; this last is a reference to the accepted rabbinic procedure in debate: the one asked a question is allowed to ask a question in return. But rather than leave things at an impasse Jesus then makes a statement which can only leave his hearers following the patterns of rabbinic exegesis to try to make out what he means.[106]

(That is), he points to the distinctive rhetorical patterns from Hebrew culture and scholarship that are essential keys in unlocking these texts more precisely.

To clarify passages like the above, scholars of the Jerusalem school, use their understanding of Hebrew culture, language, Rabbinic sources, and show how it points to a methodology used by the Sages of the Middle Ages, that dates as far back as the Babylonian exile. They suggest that Jesus used a style of teaching known as *"Pardes"* (Heb. פּרדס). The word *pardes* was:

Used as a mnemonic for the four types of biblical exegesis, an acronym of *peshat* ("the literal meaning"), *remez* ("hint," i.e., veiled allusions such as *gematria*, and *notarikon*), *derash* ("homiletically interpretation"). and *sod* ("mystery," i.e., the esoteric interpretation). The word being made up of the initial letters of these words.[107]

Lindsey uses the word "hinted" or the concept *Remez* to refer to one of the methodologies Jesus employs in the Gospel. The Hebraic background of the Gospels makes such passages difficult, but we can now translate them so that the audience can hear the words of Jesus almost like the audience of His day. Throughout the Gospels, Jesus used this method of teaching called *Remez*, when He hints or alludes to passages from the Hebrew Scriptures (Old Testament). The audiences understood, for the most part, the content of the passage He referred to. Having being trained in the study of Torah they were accustomed to such (Rabbinical) allusions.

However, our Hellenistic scholars, because of their lack of Hebraic training, are generally unable to make these connections. They misinterpret the teachings of Jesus, and how such passages clearly correlate with the Hebrew Scriptures.

The Redactor of Matthew

In this section, Matthew chapter 5:1-11, a comparison and contrast of modern New Testament commentaries with that of the Hebraic interpretation of these passages, will be given. During this commentary analysis of chapter 5, other important Hebraic styles of teaching will be employed to establish patterns that are accustomed to different kinds of speech and behavioral traditions not understood or translated correctly in New Testament commentaries.

Like the concept, "The Kingdom of Heaven," which first appears in Matthew 3:2: *And saying, Repent ye: for the kingdom of heaven is at hand,* usually the focus of scholars on this passage centers on the question: Did John preach a baptism of repentance when Matthew states that John proclaimed that the kingdom was at hand? According to Brad Young, "Matthew seems to have transferred a dominical saying and attributed it to John" (compare Matthew 4:17 and Mark 1:14-15 as well as Luke 3:3 and Mark 1:4).[108] That question remains open as Matthew continues, and comes to the fore in what is commonly known as the "Sermon on the Mount."

Matthew 5:1

Matthew 5:1: *And seeing the multitudes, he went up into a mountain: and when he was set, his disciples came unto him:*

The details behind these words expand on their significance as a set of real social practices. Donald A. Hagner, in *World Biblical Commentary*, (establishes as his theme verses 1 and 2), which he calls, *The Setting of the Sermon*, and points out in his comment that Jesus' going up into the mountain places him clearly at a "place where special events occur (4:8, the mountain of temptation; 17:1, the mountain of transfiguration, 28:16, the mountain of the resurrection appearance and the great commission)."[109] Hagner in referring to the special events that occur on the mountain, also points out that Jesus was looking to escape the crowd that accompanied Him and His disciples. However, when they 'came to Him' the event became a special time of teaching. Hagner compares the Exodus event of Moses who went up into the mountain with that of Jesus who also went up into a mountain. Finally, Hagner also supported this reading by pointing out that "it was customary in Judaism for the rabbi to teach from a seated position. Thus Jesus sat down (καθισαντος αυτου.) before He began to teach (cf. 13:2;24:3)."[110]

In Matthew 5:1, the Greek word προσηλθον is an aorist of προσερχομαι and means, "*come or go to, approach; agree with*."[111] Yet a look at the Hebrew equivalent ויגשו from the root גשׁ *to draw near* reveals the Hebraism in Semitic usage.

In Exodus 24:2 יִגַּשׁ is used to imply that Moses and Moses alone could draw near, come near, or come close to the Lord. In verse 1, the text records that Moses, along with Aaron, Nadab, Abihu, and seventy of the elders, were to come unto the Lord and worship from afar. However, it was Moses who would come into personal contact with the Lord. In Exodus 19:15 in preparation for meeting God at Mount Sinai, Moses instructs the men not to come near their wives for three days. In this verse the Hebrew words אַל־תִּגְּשׁוּ appear; clearly they were instructed not to have sexual relations with their wives. These Hebrew words therefore had a very distinct pattern of behavior associated with them, as will be noted.

Once again, understanding the Hebraic underpinnings of the gospel language allows the reader to better interpret the intent of the passage in question. The Greek word προσηλθαν has the force of future tense – as of something that will be done. The Hebrew word נָגַשׁ expresses a meaning of personal contact, such as when the disciples came into contact with Jesus. In Luke 10:9a one reads: *The Kingdom of God is near you* (NIV), and *is come nigh unto you* (KJ). In this verse the Hebrew word used for *near* or *come nigh* is קָרְבָה, and has the same meaning as the Hebrew verb נָגַשׁ. Thus the disciples were right there (in contact) taking part in the learning experience with Jesus, anticipating a change in their knowledge.

Matthew 5:2

Matthew 5:2: *And he opened his mouth, and taught them, saying,*

John Peter Lange, in *Commentary on the Holy Scriptures, Matthew*, points out that the Greek phrase ανοιξας το στομα and the Hebrew פָּתַח פֶּה are oriental and pictorial. The phrase also represents "an important element, that of confidential and solemn communication,"[112] while *A Commentary On The Old and New Testament, Matthew*, adds that the phrase *he opened his mouth* is not a superfluous statement. According to Trapp this passage seems to indicate the speaker's position as placing great importance on every word uttered.[113] But Hagner points out that the phrase has a different kind of reference associated with it, for it "is a Semitic idiom used at the beginning of a public address."[114] However, Hagner does not explain why he interprets the phrase ανοξιας το οτομα *he opened his mouth* as a Semitic idiom, or explain what the idiom means. In *The Interpreter's Bible, he opened his mouth* is interpreted as a solemn truth, a position consistent in each of the Greek New Testament commentaries. What seems to be a mere physical detail thus refers again to a convention of formal speech making or teaching in Semitic culture.

This interpretation is strengthened as the second part of the text continues. Verse 2b, *And taught them, saying*, which implies according to John Trapp, that Christians in ministry "should open their mouths with wisdom (heaven never opened in the Revelation, but some great matter followed), so their lives should be consonant to the tenor of teaching, a very visible comment on the audible word."[115] That is, he takes the passage as a metaphoric restatement reinforcing the formality and importance of the message to be communicated.

Because of their clearly formulaic nature, verses 1 and 2 have posed modern scholars a challenge that they have not taken up. Commentaries by scholars such as W. D. Davies, Dale C. Allison, Douglas R. A. Hare, W. F. Albright, and C. S. Mann, for example, do not provide any comment on these two passages. They hold the position that the text only provides a cursory interpretation of verses 1 and 2. Nevertheless, when looking at these passages in our Hebrew text we see a Jewish Jesus fully functioning in His culture of the day. For many scholars Matthew 5 might as well begin with verse 3, and yet verses 1 and 2 provide a deeper understanding of who and what was about to take place on the mountain between Jesus and His disciples.

Hagner was correct when he used the phrase "he opened his mouth" as being a Semitic idiom, and that there are clear parallels found in Exodus 13:9, *And it shall be for a sign unto thee upon thine hand, and for a memorial between thine eyes, that the Lord's law may be in thy mouth,* and in Isaiah 53:7, *He was oppressed, and he was afflicted, yet he opened not his mouth.* Both Exodus and Isaiah illustrate an idiomatic antitype found in the Hebrew Scriptures, which becomes the type employed by Jesus in the Gospels. Remember that in Matthew 5:1 the disciples come unto Him. And in verse 2, the text records that he taught them. Trapp in his commentary was also correct when he records that a traditional custom among the rabbis, was the saying: "among the Jews the Rabbis sat, the term וישב or the *sitter*, the scholar, מתאבק or one that lieth along in the dust, a token of the scholar's humility, subjecting himself even to the feet of his teacher."[116]

Trapp's reference to the *sitter* was partly correct: this concept is pure Hebraic. However, the precise translation is to *sit at the feet*, as in to sit at the feet of a Sage or Rabbi or in this case sit at the feet of the Master Jesus – this is a specific Hebrew idiom. The meaning of this idiom developed during the early stages of the peripatetic Rabbis. The tradition was based upon a Rabbi/Teacher who would travel from town to town teaching or taking on work as teacher in different households. When a Rabbi displayed skills in the hermeneutics of Torah, individuals followed him from place to place or town to town. It was also customary in the land of Israel that the roads were covered with dust, thus the saying "to eat the dust of the Rabbis feet," told the story of how many students were following the teacher. In *The Saying of the Fathers*, Aboth 1:4, for example, one finds the statement: "Jose b. Joezer of Zeredah and Jose b. Johanan of Jerusalem received [the Law] from them. Jose b. Joezer of Zeredah said Let thy house be a meeting-house for the Sages and sit amid the dust of their feet and drink in their words with thirst."[117] Thus in Matthew verses 1 and 2, we see the tradition of a peripatetic teacher being reinforced in the life style of Jesus, as He traveled throughout the land of Judea teaching his disciples.

In the Hebraic tradition, a good teacher had many disciples. It was not surprising to see those coming to follow the greatest of teachers of that day, Jesus. Those who followed were called disciples. The Greek word for disciple is μαθνται or μαθητνς, and is defined as: pupil, apprentice. This status existed in contrast to that of the teacher. Members of the new religious community, the martyrs, were such apprentices for "as long as a Christian's blood has not been shed, he is only a beginner in discipleship.[118] When the disciples came to him, he εεδιδασκες from διδωμι which is ordinarily translated as *taught*. Yet this Greek word carries the meaning of *giving someone some (of the substance)*, with "give" having in the sense "grant, bestow, impart, give a new commandment, speak plainly or intelligibly, and give an instruction."[119]

The Hebrew words in this text unfold a clear under-standing of the situation and a parallel meaning of words in the passages. The word for disciples in the Hebrew text is תלמידיו from תלמיד, simply defined as *his students* or *student*. Yet the word for taught in verse 2 of the Hebrew text, is וילמד from the root word למד and is defined as *to study* or *learn*. Taken together, they point to a different underlying scene: in the tradition of Semitic culture, the Rabbi gathers *students* who follow him from place to place, sitting at his feet or eating the dust of his feet while being taught Torah. Jesus was placed in this same Hebraic traditional setting according to Matthew's redactor: he came along gathering students, teaching them his interpretation of Torah.

93

NOTES FOR CHAPTER 4

[99]Young, *Jesus and His Jewish Parables*, p. 131: "Hans-Herbert Stoldt's important work, History and Criticism of the Marcan Hypothesis, not only questions the evidence amassed to prove Marcan priority but also studies the intellectual situation of German New Testament scholarship that gave rise to the two document theory as a working hypothesis. A careful reading of Stoldt's scholarship underscores the need to re-examine the whole question of synoptic relationships. General scholarly consensus should never be translated too rapidly into fact. Marcan priority is at best a theory, and as a theory it must stand upon its own merits and must be evaluated according to the evidence. Is the evidence for the priority of Mark conclusive? Not all students of the gospels feel comfortable with the strict application of the two document hypothesis."

[100]G. D. Kilpatrick, *The Origins of the Gospel According to St. Matthew* (Oxford: The Carendon Press, 1946) p. 3.

[101]Kilpatrick, p. 3.

[102]Kilpatrick, pp. 3-4.

[103]Young, *Jesus and His Jewish Parables*, p. 147: "The gospel of Mark cannot and should not be minimized in any consideration of the synoptic problem. The close literary interrelationships between the three earliest gospels is not disputed. However at times a tendency can be observed to emphasize the importance of the originality of Mark to the extent that the possibility that either Matthew or Luke might preserve a more reliable part of a traditions is excluded. Each text must be carefully considered and the danger of establishing avoided and will lead to fragmentary results."

[104]Young, *Jesus and His Jewish Parables*, p. 148.

[105]Lindsey, p. XX.

[106]Lindsey, p. XXI: "The Son of Man" is a Messianic title they know full well from Daniel 7:13, 14 and the "seated at the right hand" they easily identify as a reference to Messianic Psalms 110. Jesus' expression "the Power" is another accommodation to the rabbinic habit of replacing an ordinary name for the deity by an evasive synonym. But of even more interest is the seeming addition in the priestly expression "the son of God." Here, as Professor Flusser once pointed out to me, the explanation seems to be in the way the rabbis connected Psalm 2 by reading verse 3 of the former as טל ילדך (cf. the LXX) which is the same verb found n Psalm 2:7. They answer therefore: "You are then the Son of God!" and of course mean, "You are, then, the Messiah! Jesus answer, "It is you who are saying that I am he!"

[107]Eli Davis, ed. *Encyclopaedia Judaica* Vol. 13 P-Rec (Jerusalem: Keter Publishing House Jerusalem LTD 1972) p. 91.

[108]Young, *Jesus And His Jewish Parables*, p. 229: "John's ministry is certainly best understood as a revivalist

movement in which he called the people to baptism and repentance. This is a sound evaluation of the historical evidence (Jos. Ant. 18:117, Mt 3:6, Mk 1:5; Lk 3:10-14; Mt 11:4; Mk 6:18). No doubt this is one reason that he received the appellation 'John the Baptizer.' It is easy to understand how a saying of Jesus would have been attributed to John. For a different understanding of Luke 3:3, see H. Conzelmann, *The Theology of St. Luke* (Philadelphia: Fortress, 1961), p. 23 and see note 1. Conzelmann tried to show that Luke had a motive in trying to say that Jesus was the first to proclaim the kingdom. In Luke John is thought of as quite proclaimed the kingdom."

[109] Donald A. Hagner, *Word Biblical Commentary: Matthew 1-13*, Volume 33a (Dallas, Texas: Word Books, Publisher 1993) pp. 85, 86.

[110] Hagner, p. 86.

[111] Kurt Aland, Matthew Black, Carlo M. Martini, Bruce M. Metzger, and Allen Wikgren, *The Greek New Testament* (West Germany: Biblia-Druck Gmbh Stuttgart, 1966) p. 153.

[112] John Peter Lange, *Commentary on the Holy Scriptures, Matthew*, ed. Philip Schaff (Grand Rapids Michigan: Zondervan Publishing House, 1882) p. 101: "This applies especially to the moment when the Incarnate Word opened His mouth to enunciate the eternal principles of the New Covenant. We note here the contrast, as between Sinai and the Mount of Beatitudes, the law and the Gospel, so also between the speaking of God during the Old Testament, accompanied as it then was by thunder and lightning, and Jesus "opening His mouth" under the New Testament."

[113] John Trapp, *A Commentary on the Old and New Testament*, Volume Five: Matthew (Eureka, California: Tanski Publications, 1997) p. 44.

[114]Hagner, p. 86.

[115]Trapp, p. 44.

[116]Trapp, p. 44.

[117]Herbert Danby, *The Mishnah* (Oxford: Oxford University Press, 1933) p. 446.

[118]Walter Bauer, *Greek-English Lexicon of The New Testament and Other Early Christian Literature*, (Chicago and London: The University of Chicago Press, 1958) pp. 485-86.

[119]Bauer, pp. 192-93.

CHAPTER 5

THE BEATITUDES: MATTHEW 5:3-6

Matthew 5:3

Matthew 5:3: *Blessed are the poor in spirit: for theirs is the kingdom of heaven.*

W. F. Albright and C. S. Mann, in *The Anchor Bible, Matthew,* translate the Greek Μακαριοι as *fortunate,* rather than the more familiar *blessed,* and point out that this word was used in classical times of the state of the gods in contrast to men.[120] This distinction between the state of a human being and the god's points to an older Hebraic-Greek sense of how the world was divided. And yet in this older layer, another level of distinction can be drawn. The Hebrew word אשרי, *Ashre* according to Albright and Mann, originally meant "the good omens of," and they assert that it carries the same meaning as the pagan Greek word. According to Douglas R. A. Hare, in *Matthew, Interpretation,* Μακαριοι gradually became a secular way of saying "how fortunate is" or "how lucky are the wealthy."[121] In his commentary, Hare, like most scholars in the modernized, Hellenistic tradition, approach this passage from the Greek text. However, Hare, like other New Testament scholars, displayed some knowledge of the Hebrew Scripture as he writes:

> The meaning he intended in the original beatitudes undoubtedly reflects the function of *ashre* in the Hebrew Scriptures, for example, Ps. 1:1, where the happiness is less subjective than objective. The man or woman who walks not in the counsel of the wicked but delights in the law may or may not be happy in the sense in which this word is normally used in the secular world. The happiness derives from a right relationship with God (cf. Ps. 33:12, where such happiness is attributed collectively to the nation whose God is the Lord). For this reason it is probably better to retain "blessed" as the English rendering because of the word's religious associations.[122]

In the above statement Hare allows various suppositional beliefs to skew his interpretation on how the Semitic background of the word *Ashre* is used.

Hare strongly places the word "blessed" in a Hellenistic religious setting; however, in his commentary on this passage, Hagner contends:

> Although the word μακαριοι, which appears as the first word in each of the nine beatitudes, occurs in Hellenist literature, where it describes those of good fortune, the true background to the NT use of the word is the OT (Zimmeril finds forty-six instances in the Hebrew canon). The LXX often used the word as a translation

of אַשְׁרֵי (deeply "happy, blessed"). The word is of course especially appropriate in the NT in such contexts as the present one, where it describes the nearly incomprehensible happiness of those who participate in the kingdom announced by Jesus. Rather than happiness in its mundane sense, it refers to the deep inner joy of those who have long awaited the salvation promised by God and who now begin to experience its fulfillment. The μακαριοι are the deeply or supremely happy.[123]

Remember that μακαριοι is defined as "blessed, fortunate, happy. In this sense, a privileged recipient of divine favor."[124] The Hebrew word אַשְׁרֵי, from the root word אָשַׁר denotes "happiness, blessedness of"[125] as seen in I Kings 10:8: *Happy are thy men, happy are these thy servants, which stand continually before thee, and that hear thy wisdom.* Another parallel appears in Psalms 119:1-2: (Happy) *Blessed are the undefiled in the way, who walk in the law of the Lord.* (Happy) *Blessed are they that keep his testimonies, and that seek him with the whole heart.* That is, the original terminology in the Hebrew text refers to the individual's spiritual (almost psychological) state, rather than to a state of his fate or earthly condition.

Historically, there is an alternate foundation for interpreting the meaning of "blessed" preceded the LXX rendering of אַשְׁרֵי. Nevertheless, most New Testament scholars favor translating "blessed" in a Hellenistic setting, rendering the attitude of a follower of Jesus as *fortunate* (referring to an outward condition) instead of *happy* or having *happiness*. This position is best illustrated with Trapp's words: the word signifieth such as are set out of the reach of evil, in a most joyous condition, having just cause to be everlastingly merry.[126] In the commentary *The Renaissance New Testament*, Randolph O. Yeager offers a more modern theological characterization of the difference between *fortunate* μακαριοι and *happy* אשרי by combining these two words with respect to their Hebraic sense. Stressing the internal spiritual references of the term, Yeager argues, "Each characteristic is followed by the promise of a reward. Hence there is perfect character and perfect blessedness (happiness) for those who fulfill the requirements of this model."[127] However, Robert Lindsey who takes a clear Hebraic position, asserts that the term *ashrei* also represents a specific group of individuals who are now experiencing the comfort of being in and a part of Jesus' movement, called "The Kingdom of Heaven."

It is also important to point out that "the term 'happy' is often used to translate the Beatitudes instead of the word 'blessed.'"[128] Thus the Greek word *makarios* according to Young denotes approval or affirmation as in those who experience God's favor with joy. It is possible that the term in question simply denotes a condition in which those who are a part of Jesus' movement experience.

In verse 3, the context of Hebraic teaching becomes more relevant as the phrase *poor in spirit* is analyzed. Because of its Semitic background, this verse also posed theological problems for most New Testament scholars. For example, in *Jesus of Nazareth, King of the Jews*, Paula Fredriksen states, "Jesus is drawn especially to the poor, whose very poverty enriches them spiritually."[129] Albright and Mann's position is very close to that of Fredriksen as they provide an example of this point by defining poor in spirit as beggars in spirit; they write:

> Such as have nothing at all of their own to support them, but being nittily needy, and not having (as we say) a cross wherewith to bless themselves, get their living by begging, and subsist merely upon

alms. Such beggars God hath always about him, Matt. Xxvi 11.[130]

Yeager continues his interpretation by focusing on the word poor as "underprivileged," unlike the Pharisees and Sadducees who were privileged. Now, according to Yeager, Jesus turns the table and declares that those of an intellectual poverty of spirit, the babes, the fools, are the ones making up his kingdom. Such varied positions demonstrate clearly that this Semitic phrase has caused misunderstanding among New Testament academics. According to Paula Fredriksen, Jesus is also addressing Himself to those who are living without the ability to provide for themselves. She, like so many Christians, believe Jesus came to establish a ministry to meet the need of those He called the poor. This is a complete misinterpretation of the message being taught by Jesus.

It is not surprising these scholars pay great attention to the Semitic parallels of the text and yet, came up with different interpretations on this passage. For example, John Peter Lange expresses a position opposite of that by Yeager, by saying that "the expression does not imply poverty of spirit in reference to man, far less intellectual poverty."[131] And while Craig S. Keener, in *A Commentary on the Gospel of Matthew* offers a purely theological interpretation rather than the more historical-sociological one pursued here, he clarifies this point when he writes:

The expression "poor in spirit" (5:5) refers not to those with a deficit of moral righteousness (see 5:20), but reflects Matthew's explanation of the sense of Q's "poor" (Lk 6:20; see further Gundry 1982: 67). Because the oppressed poor became wholly dependent on God (Jas 2:5), some Jewish people used the title as a positive religious as well as economic designation (1QM 11.9, 13; 13.14; 14.7; 1QpHab 12.3, 6, 10; 4QpPs 37 fr. 1, 2.100.) Thus it refers not merely to the materially poor and oppressed, but to those "who have taken that condition to their very heart, by not allowing themselves to be deceived by the attraction of wealth" (Freyne 1988: 72). Although Matthew does not stress renunciation of possessions to the same degree as Luke, for him as well the kingdom belongs to the powerless of the world, to the oppressed who embrace the poverty of their condition by trusting in God rather than favors from the powerful for their deliverance.[132]

Thus Albright and Mann translate *poor in spirit* as *humble in spirit* and point out that the phrase appears in the Qumran text as *'aniye ruah*. They also point out the phrase represents "those living in uprightness, or perfection."[133] In these cases, they thus point to a culture more concerned with spiritual welfare than with material goods, which is less Hellenistic in its position. It is also noted that the term "poor in spirit" was found among the Dead Sea community, who referred to their members as "poor in spirit."[134]

Also in verse 3, the phrase *for theirs is the kingdom of heaven* offers more theological and exegetical challenges. In Hagner's commentary the good news came to the poor, and thus he interprets, that the kingdom was *theirs*. The question scholars should ask is, did Jesus intend for His followers to possess the kingdom? Here again, a language question comes into play. Bivin and Blizzard answer the language question by arguing their position, saying:

Theirs is a classic mistranslation, still preserved in all modern English versions. The Greek word translated "theirs" should be translated "of these" or "of such as these." We cannot possess the Kingdom. It does not belong to us; rather, Jesus is describing in these beatitudes the kind of people who make up the Kingdom. It is the "poor in spirit," the spiritually "down and outers" who have no righteousness of their own; "the mourners," the brokenhearted who have reached the end of their strength and cry out to God in despair and hopelessness; "the meek," those who have thrown away their pride. It is people such as these who get into the Kingdom and find salvation.[135]

It is important to note that the above statement points to the Hebrew thought and culture; "the Dead Sea community referred to its members or disciples as 'poor in spirit.'" Thus according to Young, "Clearly Jesus also designated his own followers in the same terms."[136]

The Hebraic interpretation of these phrases can be better understood by comparing them with other passages from the Hebrew Scriptures. For example, Isaiah 66:2 reads: *For all those things hath mine hand made, and all those things have been, saith the Lord: but to this man will I look, even to him that is poor and of a contrite spirit, and trembleth at my word.* In this passage a *contrite spirit* parallels *poor in spirit* in Matthew 5:3. Similarly Isaiah 57:15 reads: *For thus saith the high and lofty One that inhabiteth eternity, whose name is Holy; I dwell in the high and holy place, with him also that is of a contrite and humble spirit, to revive the spirit of the humble, and to revive the heart of the contrite ones.* Psalms 51:17 offers: *The sacrifices of God are a broken spirit: a broken and a contrite heart.* Psalms 34:18 records: *The Lord is close to the brokenhearted and saves those who are crushed in spirit.* In the above passages, contrite in spirit, humble in spirit, brokenhearted in spirit, and crushed in spirit, are all synonymous terms relating to poor in spirit.

Clearly, the phrase עֲנִיֵּי רוּחַ 'aniye ruah in verse 3 refers to a people who are emotionally and spiritually contrite, humble, broken, crushed (poor). According to Jesus, the word *theirs* in Matthew 5:3 represents those to whom "The Kingdom of Heaven" is available. Happy/Blessed are those who are spiritually broken because of life's circumstances. For they are those who are ruled by God, they make up his Kingdom, and his promises are available for them. Brad Young also writes concerning Matthew 5:3 saying:

> According to the Gospels, Jesus teaches that the kingdom is (1) God's reign among people who have chosen to obey God's commands (e.g., Matt 6:33); (2) God's power as manifest in his redemptive purpose of healing and salvation (e.g., Luke 11:20); and (3) the people who have become disciples of Jesus in the movement to bring God's redemption into the world (e.g., Matt 5:3ff.). Each individual chooses God's rule and accepts his authority. God moves dramatically in supernatural redemptive acts. His kingdom is seen at the miraculous deliverance of the people of Israel from Egypt.
>
> The kingdom is a present reality for those people who choose to obey the teachings of Jesus, to accept God's redemptive power in their lives, and to exemplify the qualities of discipleship and servant hood in a hurting and needy world. The kingdom is here![137]

A contemporary Hebraic translation of Matthew 5:3 might read: *Happy are those who are emotionally and spiritually broken, those who are crushed, or humble in spirit, and who tremble at God's word, for they are the ones for whom the Kingdom of Heaven (spiritual/supernatural) is available.*

Matthew 5:4

Matthew 5:4: *Blessed are they that mourn: for they shall be comforted.*

Donald A. Hagner renders this beatitude in close association with Isaiah 61:2. The text reads: *To proclaim the acceptable year of the Lord, and the day of vengeance of our God; to comfort all that mourn.* In Hagner's commentary he writes:

> In the second beatitude we have an even more striking allusion to the words of Isa. 61. In the LXX of Isa. 61.2, the one anointed by the Spirit says he has come παρακαλεσαι παντας τους πενθουντασ "to comfort all those who mourn." Here the key word πενθουντας. is exactly the same as in the beatitude. Thus again we find the eschatological expectation of the downtrodden and poor, those who suffer. The rabbis accordingly referred to the Messiah as the "Comforter" (*Menahem*) because of his mission in the messianic age (cf. Str-B 1:195). Those who mourn do so because of the seeming slowness of God's justice. But they are now to rejoice, even in their troubled circumstances, because their salvation has found its beginning. The time draws near when they shall be comforted (cf. Rev. 7:17; 21:4), but they are already to be happy in the knowledge that the kingdom has arrived. Their salvation is at hand. The verb παρακληθησονται is a so-called divine passive, which assumes God as the acting subject (so too in the fourth, fifth, and seventh beatitudes).[138]

The above interpretation is common among most New Testament scholars, who prefer to stress God's activity.

W. D. Davies and *The Gospel According to Saint Matthew* make this text a parallel to Isaiah 61:1:[139] "the Spirit of the Lord is upon me, because the Lord has anointed me, to preach good news, (ευαγγελισασθαι to the poor, πτωχις.") Davies and Allison interpret Isaiah 61:1 in these words: "the connection is all the surer since, in the synoptic tradition, 'to preach good news' or 'good news' is so closely bound to the kingdom of God."[140] They further buttress their claim by stating:

> The most persuasive allusions to Isa. 61 occur in 5.3,4, and in these three verses (from Q or Qmt) the links with Isa. 61 do not appear in the redactional contributions of Matthew (see for details the commentary on the individual verses). Moreover, since the allusion to Isa. 61.1 in v. 5 (from Qmt) is weaker than the allusions in vv. 3 and 4,5, the strongest links with Isa 61 are to be assigned not to Qmt but to an earlier stage of Q. So the farther back we go the greater the impact of Isa. 61 seems to be. The implication? If, as seems overwhelmingly probable, the core of the beatitudes (5.3,4,6) be dominical, Jesus must have formulated them with Isa. 61, 1-3 in mind.[141]

The approach of Davies and Allison clearly embraces the Greco-Roman school of thought in their interpretation of Matthew 5:3. To state, "Jesus must have formulated them with Isa. 61: 1-3" is clear evidence of their misinterpretation of Matthew 5:3 and following. Their basic thesis speaks to the future coming of "The Kingdom of Heaven." They do not refer to the Hebrew Scriptures and Semitic sources; instead they assert: "when Jesus employed Isa. 61 in order to bless the poor who heard him speak and promised them participation in God's eschatological kingdom, he was using the text as others had before him."[142] It would appear Davies and Allison are alluding to the prophets and merely 61:1 refers to an eschatological kingdom.

Yet the commentary strategy employed by Hagner, Davies, and Allison resembles the Hebraic style of teaching when they *hint* about the passages in Isaiah 66:1 and 2. Neither of these scholars appears to understand the concept of *Remez* or *Hinting* in the sense of a specific teaching tool that Jesus employed. Nevertheless, they alluded to the Scriptures found in Isaiah 66, possibly because this text used the words *mourn and poor*. They fail however, to incorporate Isaiah 66:3: *To appoint unto them that mourn in Zion, to give unto them beauty for ashes, the oil of joy for mourning, the garment of praise for the spirit of heaviness; the planting of the Lord, that he might be glorified.* This additional reference expresses a gesture of comforting to those who mourn. They again miss the interpersonal, psychological dimension available in a Hebraic reading of the text.

Robert Lindsey offers an important point regarding a Greek interpretation of this passage. He argues that the syntax in the first part of Matthew 5:3 is in the present tense and easily translates into English from the Greek. However, the second part of this verse is in the future tense as in "they shall be comforted."[143] According to Lindsey, the key to understanding the beatitudes is to realize that they are typical Hebrew proverbs, cast in present tense. The present tense in future allows the reader to see the beatitude of Matthew chapter 5 as proverbial truism. Hellenistic scholars on the other hand, not having any background in Hebraic culture, miss the simple message being taught that applies to everyday life and embrace a condition of truism.

The Hebrew word האבלים from the root אבל denotes *mourn* or *lament*. In the Hebrew Scriptures אבל is used closely with the idea of justice or judgment. In Hosea 10:4-5, we read: *They have spoken words swearing falsely in marking a covenant: thus judgment springeth up as hemlock in the furrows of the field. The inhabitants of Samaria shall fear because of the calves of Beth-aven: for the people thereof shall mourn over it.*

The above passage conveys normal conditions which the people faced every day. Here their mourning is based upon their actions. That is, their emotional state has resulted from what they did, and it is expressed as very ordinary, when the passage refers to calves and field furrows. In Amos 8:8, all the people mourn and are judged based upon two conditions. First, there are those who mourn because of the suffering they have caused in the lives of the poor and needy; they mourn in wait of their judgment. Second, there are those who are the oppressed (the poor, the needy) upon whom others imposed suffering. These people mourn and are comforted when God's justice comes. Such is the case with those of Matthew 5:4: they are to be happy, knowing that in their suffering they are comforted. Note, however, that this comfort depends on justice – a state of mind and spirit, which is in contrast to the state of civil justice.

One additional comparison can be made to clarify the tense within this passage. In Matthew 5:4 the Hebrew word ינחמו from the root נחם *to comfort* or *comforting* can also be understood as *compassion*. In Isaiah 57:18, *I have seen his ways, and will heal him: I will lead him also, and restore comforts unto him and to his mourners*, the Hebrew text states ואנחהו ואשלם נחמים לו ולאבליו *I will lead him and restore comfort to him and his mourners*. Comfort in this verse implies compassion. In the Semitic tradition Jesus taught his students saying, happy are those who mourn for they get comforted. More important for us is the meaning of *happiness, mourning,* and *comfort*; these are not only emotional words, they also refer to legal and social status. In the above passage Jesus not only points to spiritual comfort, He also points to social justice as well, as proclaimed by Job in chapter 29:16a, *I took up the case of the stranger.*[144]

A contemporary Hebraic translation of Matthew 5:4 might thus read: *Happy are those who mourn (those who cry out for God's help), for they get comforted.*

Matthew 5:5

Matthew 5:5: *Blessed are the meek: for they shall inherit the earth.*

Here, again, there is a sense of the passage hidden behind conventional Hellenized readings. John Lange's interpretation provides an excellent example of Greek mindset which at the time forced a conclusion completely separate from our Hebrew text. Lange writes:

The meek – Ps. Xxxvii. 11, according to the Septuagint: οι δε πραεις κληρονομηουσιν γην They who suffer in love, or love in patience; they who, in the strength of love, boldly yet meekly, meekly yet boldly, bear injustice, and thereby conquer. In this beatitude, the promise of the Holy Land (the enemies being driven out) is a symbol of the kingdom of heaven; still, outward possession, and that in all its faultless, is also referred to in the expression: the *land,* the *earth.*[145]

In the above statement, Lange offers a theological interpretation of "meek"; he provides no definition of being meek in practical terms or real behavior. Instead he sees the Beatitudes as theological principles, rather than in relation to real-life situations. According to Lange, the Kingdom of Heaven becomes a symbol, a promise to inherit the earth or land. While the word 'meek' according to Lange, theologically takes on the meaning of those who *suffer in love,* and who in the strength of love suffer.

Donald Hagner, W. F. Albright and C. S. Mann, John Trapp, and Douglas R. A. Hare agree that Matthew 5:5 is parallel to Psalms 37:11: *But the meek shall inherit the earth*. Hagner points out that the Greek phrase ιο δε πραεις κληρονομησονσιν "the meek shall inherit the earth" is a passage in which the Hebrew word עֲנָוִים *'ananwim* underlies the Greek word πραεις. He also points out that in Isaiah 61:1 the Greek word for poor, πραεις is also translated as poor in LXX, and "therefore we have approximately the same thought here as in the first beatitude."[146] To stress the importance of this parallel, Hagner makes an interesting statement concerning the syntax order of Matthew 5. He writes:

> The beatitude stands in parallel with the assertion of the first beatitude that the kingdom of heaven belongs to the poor in spirit. It is possible, though we cannot be certain, that the third beatitude originally followed the first in synonymous parallelism and that the evangelist broke the couplet by inserting the beatitude concerning those who mourn, in order to follow the lead of Isa. 61:1-2 (thus Guelich, *Sermon*, 82). See *Form/Structure/ Setting*, above. It should be noted that the LXX of Isa. 61:7 also contains the word κληρονομησονσιν την γην "they will inherit the land (earth)."[147]

In the above statement, Hagner correctly parallels verses 1 and 3. However, he concludes that the redactor inserted verse 2 following the lead of Isaiah 61:1-2, and that in the original text verse 3 should have followed verse 1. His argument that verse 2 was an insertion, based on Isaiah 61:1-2, is completely misleading, and a lack of understanding of the Semitic background of the first century.

Albright and Mann simply interpret *the meek* as "humble" or "poor" and implied "possessing the earth is parallel to being admitted to the kingdom in vs. 3."[148] However when viewing Trapp's comments it is clear his position is solely theological in nature. He argues that, "meekness is the fruit of mourning for sin, and is therefore fitly set next after it. He that can kindly melt in God's presence, will be made thereby as meek as a lamb: and if God will forgive him his ten thousand talents, he will not think much to forgive his brother a few farthings."[149] Trapp correctly contrasts the Hebrew word that signifies "afflicted" with that of "meek."

Hare provides us with another interesting Hellenistic perspective that follows the theological format of our previous comments. Hare says "the meek who will inherit the earth are nonviolent people, who are humble and gentle in their dealings with others because they have humbled themselves before the greatness of God."[150] He also embraced the concept of Kingdom as referring to the future, by stating:

> Whether this beatitude was intended to be taken so literally, however, may be doubted. Matthew himself seems to believe that the full establishment of God's kingdom will occur only after the dissolution of life as we know it (see 24:29, 38-41). He may therefore have understood "inherit the earth" as synonymous with "for theirs is the kingdom of heaven."[151]

Herein, we see another scholar's weak theological interpretation of a beautiful Hebraic proverbial saying, as a truism. Trapp and Hare are simply guessing or assuming the answer for this beatitude. The Kingdom of Heaven is to be established only after the dissolution of life occurs. Thus Hare believes the meek were to be like Moses in Numbers 12:3: *Now the man Moses was very meek*. Accordingly, for him this passage represents a description of what the recipients of the third beatitude should reflect in life.

These scholars are not alone in arguing the values of the Beatitudes as principally theological. The commentary by W. D. Davies and Dale C. Allison, *A Critical and Exegetical Commentary on the Gospel According to Saint Matthew*, is a very comprehensive and exegetical study on Matthew. Anyone in Biblical studies, whether they are convinced of the Greek or Hebrew school of thought, should agree that Davies' and Allison's academic commentary has set them apart from other New Testament scholarship. Their research is, at first look, better than any of their peers. With that in mind and with respect of their contribution, it is clear they did not understand a Hebraic text was underlying the Greek text of our Gospel.

In their commentary, Davies and Allison argue that Matthew 5:5 is based upon Psalm 37:11 and "was added by an editor of Qmt in order to explicate the first beatitude (which at one time immediately followed). The word, πραυς usually translated 'meek,' was intended to make plain the religious dimension of 'poor' (this before Matthew's qualification, 'in spirit')."[152] Interestingly, Davies and Allison offer yet another definition of the Greek word πραυς of which, according to them, the word "powerless" may be a better translation. To make their point in another way, they also argued "the πραυς are not so much actively seeking to avoid hubris (attitude) as they are, as a matter of fact, powerless in the eyes of the world (a condition).[153] In his commentary, Craig Kenner presents a work on the word meek as following:

> These are the 'poor in spirit,' 'the meek' (5:3,5; both terms possibly reflecting the same Semitic term 'anawim), which also represents humility in Sirach, the Dead Sea Scrolls, and the rabbis (Dawes 1991). Some in the Greek world praised the generosity of leaders as "meekness" (Schweizer 1975: 89; Babrius 102.3; Plut. *Brutus* 29.2) and

valued meekness in the sense of gentleness, but the concept of humility often connoted the proper attitude only toward those of inferior rank and status. Judaism, however, valued humility highly (Ps 72:2; Prov 3:34). It also condemned the wicked who trod the lowly underfoot (1 Enoch 96:5; cf. 4 Ezra 11:42).[154]

Again in the above statement, Keener repeats the error already seen by other Hellenistic scholars; he represents meek as "gentle or gentleness" and states that those who display humility are also inferior in rank and status. Kenner, like his colleagues, supports the position that verse 3 of the Beatitudes should follow verse 1; he refers to the Q source as support for his position. He further argues:

> The expression "poor in spirit" (5:5) refers not to those with a deficit of moral righteousness (see 5:20), but reflects Matthew's explanation of the sense of Q's "poor" (Lk 6:20; see further Gundry 1982: 67). Because the oppressed poor became wholly dependent on God (Jas 2:5), some Jewish people used the title as a positive religious as well as economic designation. Thus it refers not merely to the materially poor and oppressed, but to those "who have taken that condition to their very heart, by not allowing themselves to be deceived by the attraction of wealth" (Freyne 1988: 72). Although Matthew does not stress renunciation of possessions to the same degree as Luke, for him as well the kingdom belongs to the powerless of the world, to the oppressed who embrace the poverty of their condition by trusting in God rather than favors from the powerful for their deliverance.[155]

In the tradition of most Greek scholars, Keener upholds the same positions taken by Davies and Allison. He refers to the term meek as being 'gentle,' but contrasts the word 'powerless' with those who are oppressed, for such as these make up the kingdom and receive the favor of God. It would be difficult to understand in view of various biblical criticism, how these scholars could continue to mislead themselves concerning Jesus' teachings on the Beatitudes of Matthew 5. Proper application of each criticism such as Form Criticism, which aims to get back to the historical setting in which a passage originated, would call into question many of these positions being held. Which historical criticism interpreted as being meek, as the one whom God's favor is given, and in what Biblical historical setting does this phrase "God's favor" appear?

Yeager's definition of the term "meek" is closely associated with that of Keener. Yeager uses "gentle" but adds "soft" to define the Greek word meek. He does offer an interesting parallel to *poor in spirit* and *meek* in that "poor in spirit" equals a "quiet spirit." Thus a meek and quiet spirit, according to Yeager, is described as being *soft* and *gentle*, likened unto Christ in Matthew 11:29; 21:5. Yeager's germane position is further established in the following words:

> The same grammatical construction as in verse 4, except that οι πραεις is an adjectival substantive instead of participial as in verse 4. Again Messiah contradicts popular thinking about the Kingdom. It was hoped that when He came, Messiah would be a mighty militarist, who, like Gideon, would blow a trumpet in Israel, march on Rome and break the Roman yoke from Israel's neck. Meekness or softness, as πραεις may be translated, was not a quality to be desired in Messiah. Yet He speaks of it as a blessed characteristic and promises that

the meek and non-resisting should be heir to the earth. Certainly it is not a militaristic passage. Genghis Khan, Hannibal, Napoleon and Hitler apparently rejected this philosophy. They did not inherit the earth. *Cf.* Ps. 37:11. Our Lord was "meek and lowly of heart" – Mt. 11:29 and rode into Jerusalem "meek and riding on an ass" Mt. 21:5. A Christian should adorn himself with a "meek spirit" – I Pet. 3:4...Since meekness is one of the fruits of the Spirit (Gal.5:23) it is available only to the regenerate (Rom. 8:9). Thus only the regenerate children of God have a chance to inherit the earth.[156]

Again we can see how Yeager's interpretation follows the normal pattern found amongst most New Testament scholarship. In the above statement Yeager's commentary is redactic in nature. He associates being *meek* with that of a *meek spirit*. Thus, accordingly all Christians should display this attribute, which is patterned after Christ. The above interpretation can easily be used as a means to support passivism teachings.

However, concerning Matthew 5:5, Robert Lindsey, again from the Hebraic prospective, points out that this verse is parallel to verse 3. Thus the syntax of verse 5 should be understood in the syntax of verse 3. Unlike commentators who believe verse 5 should have followed verse 3 because of the close association with the words "poor of spirit" and "meek," Lindsey places the beatitudes and this passage back into its Hebraic context with the following statement:

Such sayings in Hebrew can use the imperfect, perfect or participial form of the verb. We cannot translate proverbial expressions in Hebrew as if the imperfect represented a true future or the perfect a true past. Both in Greek and English a proverbial expression must be put in the present.

Yet the Greek translator of Hebrew normally used Greek's future tense for the Hebrew perfect. In this way the proverbial form of the Hebrew is lost in translation...Without doubt one of the reasons so many scholars have supposed that Jesus was in the habit of talking about "inaugurating the Kingdom of God" or "setting it up" some time in the future was due to their failure to take Greek texts back to Hebrew where necessary.[157]

Lindsey's research in the field of Hebraic studies has set a standard for students to follow for generations to come. In the above statement, Lindsey suggests that New Testament scholars should have the ability to translate the text in both Greek and Hebrew. According to Lindsey, the mistake Greek scholars are making is translating the Hebrew imperfect tense with the Greek future tense. It is a very common mistake being made by Bible translators. Thus, according to our English translation of the Greek text Matthew 5:5, *blessed are the meek* is translated with the present tense and *for they shall inherit the earth* is translated in the future tense. However, according to Lindsey, *inheriting the earth* is parallel to *theirs is the kingdom of heaven*. And as already explained, "theirs" in Matthew 5:3 should be rendered "of these" or "of those" because the kingdom of heaven cannot be possessed. In both Matthew 5:3, and 5:5, the rendering of the text should not be futuristic as in something yet to come. The Hebraism of the text's focus is in the present tense, dealing with those who are meek, those who are poor in spirit, and those who suffer inwardly because of their daily conditions. Examples can be seen in the following passages:

Psalms 22:26: The meek shall eat and be satisfied: they shall praise the Lord that seek him: your heart shall live for ever.

Psalms 25:9: The meek will he guide in judgment: and the meek will he teach his way.

Psalms 51:17: My sacrifice [the sacrifice acceptable] to God is a broken spirit; a broken and a contrite heart [broken down with sorrow for sin, and humbly and thoroughly penitent] such, O God, You will not despise. Psalms 147:6: The Lord lifteth up the meek: he casteth the wicked down to the ground.

Psalms 149:4: For the Lord taketh pleasure in his people: he will beautify the meek with salvation.

Zephaniah 2:3: Seek ye the Lord, all ye meek of the earth, which have wrought his judgment; seek righteousness, seek meekness: it may be ye shall be hid in the day of the Lord's anger.

Isaiah 57:15: For thus saith the high and lofty One that inhabiteth eternity, whose name is Holy, I dwell in the high and holy place, with him also that is of a contrite and humble spirit, to revive the spirit of the humble, and to revive the heart of the contrite ones.

The above passages are based upon an English translation. And we see in them the same mistakes as in Matthew 5:3 and 5:5 being made. In the English translation, the tense implies only future conditions. A literal translation of the Hebrew text in Psalms 22:27 will illustrate when the present is used, and when or if the future tense is used. The Hebrew reads:

יאכלו ענוים וישבעו יהללו יהוה דרשיו יחי לבבכם לעד.

A literal translation would read *they eat, the afflicted (or meek or poor), and they are satisfied, they praise the Lord, the seekers of Him, may live your heart forever.* A natural translation would read: *the afflicted they eat, and are satisfied, the seekers of Him praise the Lord, for your hearts live forever.* Thus Psalms 37:11 states, *But the meek shall inherit the earth: and shall delight themselves in the abundance of peace*; also in verse 9 of chapter 37 it says, *For evildoers shall be cut off: but those that wait upon the Lord, they shall inherit the earth.*

One final example found n Psalm 25:9; the Hebrew text reads: ידרך במשפט ענוים דרצו A literal Hebrew translation would read: *He treads (leads) the afflicted in justice, and He teaches them that are meek, His ways.* Both passages illustrate that the Hebrew syntax is focused on the present and not the future tense. Thus Psalm 37:11 says, *But the meek shall inherit the earth: and shall delight themselves in the abundance of peace.*

A contemporary Hebraic translation of Matthew 5:5 might read: *Happy are those who are contrite in heart, who are sorrowful for their sins, who have repented and have turned to God, those who love his word and keep his commandments, those who hope and look and wait for the Lord. For they are the people over whom God is now ruling, and they are the ones who inherit the earth.*

Matthew 5:6

Matthew 5:6: *Blessed are they which do hunger and thirst after righteousness: for they shall be filled.*

Donald Hagner offers this interesting interpretation of verse 6:

In keeping with the preceding, the fourth beatitude names the literally hungry and thirsty, i.e., the downtrodden and oppressed, who especially hunger and thirst after the justice associated with the coming of God's eschatological rule. There is, then, no significant difference between the Matthean and Lukan versions of the beatitude, despite the additional words και διψιτες την δικαιοσιην "and thirst of justice," in Matthew. That δικαιοσυνη here means "justice" rather than "personal righteousness" is clear from the context. The poor, the grieving, and the downtrodden (i.e., those who have experienced injustice) are by definition those who long for God to act. They are the righteous who will inherit the kingdom. Yet this interpretation does not altogether exclude the sense of δικαιοσυνη as personal righteousness. The justice of God's eschatological rule presupposes the δικαιοσυνη of those who enjoy its blessing (cf. II Pet. 3:13). Thus, albeit to a slight degree, this verse may anticipate the stress on δικαιοσυνη in v 20 and 6:33.[158]

In this statement, Hagner associates those who *hunger and thirst* with those who are *downtrodden and oppressed*. According to Hagner, they are looking for God's justice, but unfortunately they must wait for the eschatological rule of God to come. He interprets the Greek word δικαιοσυνη as meaning "justice," and declares that the righteous just are those who inherit the kingdom. Theologically, Hagner's position is very sound: i.e., the Greek word δικαιοσυνη can also be defined as the "*uprightness, justice* as a characteristic of a Judge."[159] However, because of our position that a Hebrew text underlies the Greek manuscript, the Hebrew word in Matthew 5:6, that underlies δικαιοσυνη is צדקה *righteousness*.

In Hagner's writings, it is clear from the context of verse 6 that δικαιοσυνη takes on the meaning of *justice* rather than *personal justice/ righteousness*. The Hebrew word צדקה (righteousness) carries a range of meanings. Joseph Frankovic, in *The Kingdom of Heaven*, writes concerning the term righteousness:

> During the first century A.D., when Jews spoke a type of Hebrew known as Mishnaic Hebrew, *tsedakah* had come to mean almsgiving. For example, in Matthew 6:1 the Greek *dikaiosunae* means charitable deed. This indicates that underneath *dikaiosunae* lurks the Hebrew word *tsedakah*, because *dikaiosunae* in Classical Greek does not mean almsgiving, *Dikaiosunae* takes on this meaning when Hebrew (or Aramaic) has influenced the Greek.

Frankovic, in the above statement, points out that historically the word *righteousness* has been translated using several different English words. For example, *The New Brown-Driver-Briggs-Gesenius Hebrew and English Lexicon,* defines צדקה *tsedakah* as *vindication, salvation,* and *deliverance.*

Douglas Hare opens this part of his commentary with the words: "it is customary to regard 'righteousness' here as a reference to personal ethics...The First Gospel places heavy emphasis on personal righteousness (see 5:20; 7:21-24)."[160] However, according to Hare, two factors count against this reading:

> First, it seems a little presumptuous to understand this beatitude as promising perfect righteousness to those who work hard at achieving it (TEV: "God will satisfy them fully"). Second, the metaphors

of hungering and thirsting seem more apt with reference to a righteousness that is not subject to our willing and doing, the righteousness of God. Here we should think not of the "right-wising" righteousness of the ungodly of which Paul writes so eloquently in Romans but of God's saving righteousness as proclaimed by the prophets. "My righteousness [RSV: "deliverance"] draws near speedily, my salvation has gone forth" (Isa. 51:5). Isaiah 51:1 must be understood in the same way: "Listen to me, you that pursue righteousness [RSV: "deliverance"], you that seek the Lord" (NRSV). It is not their own righteousness that is the object of their yearning but God's.[161]

It is clear that Hare struggles with what he calls the Prophet's interpretation, one rooted in his traditional Hellenistic schooling. An example of Hare's confusion can be seen in these words:

If it is correct to understand the beatitude in this way ("Blessed are those who yearn for the manifestation of God's saving righteousness"), the distance between Luke's version and Matthew's is greatly diminished. In the Lukan parallel it is clear that this beatitude, like the first, refers to those who are literally hungry. The corresponding woe promises the well-fed that they will exchange places with the undernourished (Luke 6:21,25). Like Luke, Matthew yearns for the establishment of social justice.[162]

Hare correctly interprets the term *righteousness* as used by the Prophets and in the Hebrew Scriptures to denote God's saving acts, God's deliverance, and God's salvation.

His comparison of Matthew 5:6 with Isaiah 51:1, in contrast, was a complete misplacement of the text. Furthermore, Hare's position connected Luke 6:21 as meaning "those who literally hunger." The prophets interpreted righteousness in a spiritual manner, while Hare's interpretation centers on social justice.

The commentary by Randolph Yeager points out that there are two types of hungering and thirsting, a spiritual thirsting and a physical thirsting. The following statement clearly expresses Yeager's position:

> To the Jewish audience it probably meant the Messianic reign, when "righteousness would be the girdle of His loins" – social and political righteousness. But only those who desire personal righteousness would sincerely crave social righteousness. Where the passages with διφαω are used of spiritual thirsting. Those thus hungering and thirsting are happy because their craving shall be satisfied. The figure is a powerful one. Who has not hugely enjoyed food after prolonged hunger or a cool, sparkling glass of water, after burning thirst? So is the blessedness of one craving righteousness and finding it.[163]

This statement speaks volumes about the Hellenistic perspective that has traditionally skewed scholars' positions for years. For Yeager, this Beatitude, like the earlier ones, is a product of an eschatological belief taught in seminaries across the country. Thus the Kingdom inaugurated in the Gospels by Jesus was interpreted as a Kingdom not yet established, a Kingdom that was to come.

Accordingly Trapp states that righteousness "is in us from Christ, being wrought by his virtue and spirit, and is called the righteousness of sanctification."[164] Trapp turns to characters found in the Hebrew Scriptures expressing a type of desire in which those who are hungering and thirsting must earnestly prevail within themselves. He uses the story of Rachel who for the sake of her children would prevail or perish. And that of David who "did thirst after the water of the well of Bethlehem, to the jeopardy of the lives of his three mightiest, I Chron xi.18; as the hunted hart (or, as the Septuagint read it, ελαφοξ hind) brayeth after the water-brooks."[165] Here we have beautiful poetic words that mean absolutely nothing in regards to defining righteousness. The above words by Trapp were concluded with this saying:

> This spiritual appetite and affection ariseth from a deep and due sense and feeling of our want of Christ, whole Christ, and that there is an absolute necessity of every drop of his blood. There must be a sad and serious consideration of man's misery and God's mercy. Whence will arise (as in hunger and thirst), 1. A sense of pain in the stomach. 2. A want and emptiness. 3. An eager desire of supply from Christ, who is the true bread of life, and heavenly manna; the rock flowing with honey, and fountain of living water, that reviveth the fainting spirits of every true Jonathan and Samson, and makes them never to thirst again after the world's tasteless fooleries: Like as his mouth will not water after homely provision that hath lately tasted of delicate sustenance.[166]

Trapp does not provide even a theological interpretation of what it means to hunger and thirst for righteousness. The above statement is completely void of any biblical interpretation concerning Matthew 5:6. The fact that those who are hungering and thirsting must prevail or perish within themselves seems to have nothing to do with the words in this passage.

Davies and Allison, in the tradition of Hellenistic scholarship, exegete this passage of Matthew 5:7 very differently. They compare Psalms 107:5-7; Isaiah 49:10; 55:1-2; 65:13; John 6:35; Revelation 7:16 with verse 6, and state that "righteousness is to be earnestly and habitually sought, as though it were meat and drink."[167] They also argued that Matthew inserted the phrase *and thirst after righteousness*, as a comparison with Luke 6:21a, Blessed are ye that hunger now. According to Davies and Allison, *to hunger and thirst* after righteousness, is parallel to Matthew 6:33, those who seek *first the kingdom of God and his righteousness*. The grammatical meaning of verse 6 is not a passive longing, but active in seeking, as in his righteousness. This statement is somehow connected to a passage found in Sanhedrin 100a, which says, "*Him who starves himself for the sake of the study of Torah in this world, the Holy One, blessed be He, will fully satisfy in the next.*"[168]

The word "righteousness" is the key to understanding verse 6. However, according to Davies and Allison:

The addition of 'righteousness' serves two or perhaps three ends. (1) It clarifies the object of 'hunger,' which in Q remained unspecified. (It does not, however, simply spiritualize a physical need. Even in Luke Q 'the hungry are men who both outwardly and inwardly are painfully deficient in the things essential to life as God meant it to be, and who since they cannot help themselves, turn to God on the basis of his promise'). (2) It brings the beatitudes into closer connexion with the rest of the sermon on the mount, in which 'righteousness' is a prominent theme (5.10,20; 6.1,33). (3) Given the use of the first few verses of Isa 61 in the first three beatitudes, it is perhaps to be noted that 'righteousness' occurs in Isa 6:1-3 LXX.[169]

In the statement above, righteousness is theologically used in three ways. First, righteousness is represented as the hunger of those who are deficient inwardly and outwardly, because of the natural conditions in life. These are those who look to God's promise for their needs. Their second position is correct, yet not for the reason stated. The beatitudes verses 3-11 are themes as in a sub-title, in a sense that we can view all nine beatitudes as sub-titles without content. Davies and Allison's last position contrasts Matthew 5:6 with that of Isaiah 61:3, where the word righteousness reflects the same meaning as the first three beatitudes. They interpret the end of verse 6 by stating that righteousness was a gift from God; therefore, if righteousness is a gift from God, then those who hunger and thirst are satisfied by this righteousness. To support this claim, they refer to Matthew 5:7, by stating:

> Just as those who show mercy are given mercy (5:7), overlook the fact that a direct correspondence between character and reward does not obtain in most of the beatitudes (cf. Przybyliski, p. 97). The meek are not given meekness. The pure in heart are not given purity. The peacemakers are not given peace. It is therefore far from obvious that those who hunger and thirst for righteousness gain righteousness. And even if this were not so, the righteousness to be given would not need to be identified with justification or vindication, it could simply be interpreted as the righteousness that is to prevail in the new aeon, in which all will follow the Law of God without deviation. But the deciding factor is this: the righteousness of 5:6 should probably be construed in terms of the word's

usage elsewhere in the sermon on the mount, in 5:10, 20, 6:1, 33. And since in these places we shall find righteousness to be the right conduct required by God, such is probably the meaning here. Particularly weighty is 5:10: 'Blessed are those persecuted for righteousness sake.' Righteousness cannot, in this verse, have anything to do with divine vindication, nor can it mean justification or be God's gift. It is, rather, something disciples have, and they are persecuted because of it. Hence it is recognizable behaviour of some sort.[170]

Matthew 5:6a, *For they shall be filled,* expresses a conditional result in which those in need are satisfied. In the above statement, Davies and Allison are reflecting the Hellenistic meaning of the Greek word righteousness, δικαιοσυνη. According to Walter Bauer's *Greek-English Lexicon,* δικαιοσυνη is defined as *uprightness, justice* "in a moral and religious sense: *uprightness, righteousness,* the characteristic required of men by God...righteousness in the sense of fulfilling the divine statutes...*righteousness, uprightness* as the compelling motive for the conduct of one's whole life.[171] Theologically, and according to Bauer, righteousness here is "right standing with God." Davies and Allison of course, take the position that righteousness according to the teachings of Jesus cannot and did not mean *vindication, deliverance,* or *salvation,* according to the word's Hebraic meaning. Rather, righteousness is a gift bestowed upon those who, by God, have attained right conduct, or those who are in right standing with God. Davies and Allison strongly state that δικαιοσυνη which refers to those who were persecuted found in Matthew 5:10 is not the same *dikaiosunae* of Matthew 5:6, in which divine vindication, salvation, and justification came from God.

The Semitic background of this passage can be seen in how it parallels with verses 3, 4, and 5. Those who are *poor in spirit, they who mourn,* and those who are *meek,* are also the same as those who *hunger and thirst for righteousness.* Bivin and Blizzard offer a Hebraic meaning of the word righteousness in the following:

> In Hebrew, there are many synonyms for "salvation." The word "salvation" itself is little used. Other words express this concept more powerfully. "Righteousness" is one of the synonyms for "salvation." Zion is called "the city of *righteousness*" (Isaiah 1:26). The branch of David is called "The Lord is our *righteousness*" (Jeremiah 23:6, 33:16). In great distress, David asks God to pour out His wrath on his enemies: "Let them not come into Your *righteousness*. May they be blotted out of the book of life, and not be recorded with the righteous" (Psalm 69:27-28). Jesus exhorts his disciples to "seek first the Kingdom of Heaven and His *righteousness*" (Matthew 6:33). Of such people is the Kingdom of Heaven made up.[172]

Instead of interpreting verse 6a *Blessed are they which do hunger and thirst after righteousness* as a natural condition in which the individual is physically hungry and thirsty, Bivin and Blizzard correctly interpret hunger and thirst for righteousness as a spiritual condition in which the individuals get spiritually satisfied. An example can be seen in these words, the Lord is our salvation, the Lord is our vindication, the Lord is our deliverer, and the Lord is our justice. Each of the above clauses are synonymous meanings for the Hebrew word righteousness. Thus, righteousness in the biblical text is a way of life in which God's people, who made covenant, promised to display this attribute each day as they live for the Lord.

A contemporary Hebraic translation of Matthew 5:6 might therefore read: *Blessed are those hungering and those thirsting (who are crying out for God's redemption, salvation for righteousness), for they get satisfied.*

NOTES FOR CHAPTER 5

[120]W. F. Albright and C. S. Mann, *The Anchor Bible*, Matthew (Garden City New York: Doubleday & Company, Inc. 1971) p. 45: "The usual English 'blessed' has more and more come to have liturgical or ecclesiastical overtones, and we have chosen 'fortunate' as being the best translation available to us."

[121]Douglas R. A. Hare, *Matthew, Interpretation* (Louisville: John Knox Press, 1949) p. 35: "It is difficult to find an adequate translation for the word makarioi, the first word in each of the beatitudes. In Homer's Greek it was used to describe the immortals of Mount Olympus...On the basis of the secular usage, some modern translations and commentators render the word as 'happy' as, for example, TEV: 'Happy are the pure in heart' (5:8). It is even suggested that the original force of the word would be better captured in English by rendering it as 'congratulation' – 'Congratulations to pure in heart because they are going to see God!'"

[122] Hare, pp. 35-36.

[123] Hagner, p. 91.

[124] Bauer, p. 486.

[125] Brown, Drivers, Briggs, pp. 80-81.

[126] Trapp, p. 44: "And ministers should (as Gideon's soldiers) carry trumpets of sound doctrine in one hand and lamps of good living in the other. There should be a happy harmony, a constant consent between their lips and their lives."

127. Randolph O. Yeager, *The Renaissance New Testament Vol 1* (Bowling Green, Kentucky: Renaissance Press, Inc. 1976) p. 331: "Translation – Happy are the intellectually humbled, because to them belongs the kingdom of the heaven."

[128] Brad H. Young, *Jesus The Jewish Theologian*, (Peabody, Massachusetts: Hendrickson Publishers, 1995) p. 91: "In my opinion this translation is unfortunate and has little foundation. The Hebrew term ashrei (which is translated into Greek by makarios) "blessed" should not be rendered as "happy." Happiness is not the same as joy. But the word ashre comes from a root that refers to affirmation, acceptance, or favor which is often accompanied by joy and happiness as well as physical well-being and material blessing. Probably the term would be better understood as denoting divine affirmation of approval. It has a spiritual meaning that goes beyond modern views of happiness. A man or a woman who is "blessed" possesses the well-being which accompanies God's favor. He or she has received divine acceptance and blessing. One possesses a sense of belonging to God as well as his affirmation. I much prefer the translation "blessed." For the rich Hebrew background of the word "blessed," consider the use of the term in the context of the Psalms or the story of utter joy associated with the divine favor given at the birth of a child (e.g., Gen 30:13)."

[129]Paula Fredriksen, *Jesus of Nazareth, King of the Jews* (New York: Vintage Books A Division of Random House, Inc. 1999) p. 103: "Indeed, as we have just seen, he enjoins care of the poor and an ethic of voluntary poverty on his followers. Jesus puts membership in and obligations to his group above normal ties to family and property."

[130]Albright and Mann, p. 44.

[131]Lange, p. 102: "The poor in spirit, oi ptwcoi tw pneumati – The dative is here used to designate them more particularly: in their spirit, or in reference to their spirit or spiritual life; those who feel themselves spiritually poor, and hence realize their deep and inexpressible want of the Spirit, and long for the religion of the Spirit."

[132]Craig S. Keener, *A Commentary on the Gospel of Matthew* (Grand Rapids, Michigan: William B. Eerdmans Publishing Company 1960) pp. 168-169.

[133]Albright and Mann, p. 46: "There are two words in Hebrew which would provide us with the background for this saying: 'anavim and 'aniyim. They are virtually synonymous, and both mean 'poor,' 'afflicted,' 'humble.'"

[134]Young, p. 86. "As a result of the discovery of the Dead Sea Scrolls, we have strong evidence that Jesus also designated his disciples with this term 'poor in spirit.' These words alluded to a rich biblical heritage which possessed profound significance for Jesus' Jewish disciples. The social context of the Beatitudes then may be identified in Jesus' disciples. They are blessed. They possess divine approval and affirmation. But they must strive to live up to their description."

[135]Bivin and Blizzard, pp. 81-82: "In the opening beatitude Jesus couples 'poor in spirit' with 'kingdom of heaven.' 'Poor in spirit' is an abbreviation of 'poor and crippled in spirit' in Isaiah 66:2. The Kingdom of Heaven is what Jesus calls the body of his followers, his movement. In

Hebrew, 'kingdom' can mean 'rule' or 'those who are ruled,' but it is never a territorial designation. 'Heaven' is an evasive synonym for 'God.'"

[136]Young, p. 86. "The first of the Beatitudes should be translated as a partitive genitive rather than a possessive. It is better to translate, 'Blessed are the poor in spirit, for from them is the kingdom of heaven.' This is the partitive genitive idea. The possessive genitive translation is more widely used, 'Blessed are the poor in spirit, for theirs is the kingdom of heaven.' But the poor in spirit do not own or possess the kingdom. They make up the kingdom. The disciples of Jesus comprise the movement spearheading the force of the divine rule in the lives of people experiencing God's favor." p. 92.

[137]Young, p. 81: "Modern interpreters have sometimes missed the message of the kingdom of heaven. It is not about the future age. The kingdom is not heaven in the sense that someone dies to enter in. It is neither the church nor a denomination. It is not given over to human leaders for their custodial care. Jesus did not view the kingdom as a political ideology or program. The kingdom is a process which cannot be imposed upon others through political activism. The kingdom comes by God alone. It is a divine force in the world that brings healing to suffering humanity. Hence, Jesus did not define the kingdom in terms of the future. The kingdom has precedent. When God worked the miracle of the exodus, the people sang that his reign is forever and ever (Exod 15:19). The miracles of the Bible reveal the sovereignty of God. In the mind of Jesus, the kingdom is repeatable because he taught his disciples to continue his work of mending the world. For Jesus and his early followers, the kingdom of heaven was a strong force in their personal lives which is experienced in the present age."

[138]Hagner, p. 92.

[139]I have discussed this issue in my 2000 M.A. Thesis entitled "The Kingdom of Heaven In Rabbinic Literature and The Gospel of Matthew," for the University of Texas at Austin (December 2000), pp. 72-73.

[140]W. D. Davies and Dale C. Allison, *A Critical and Exegetical Commentary on the Gospel According to Saint Matthew* (59 George Street: T. & T. Clark Limited, 1988) p. 436.

[141]Davies and Allison, p. 438: "Two observations confirm the conclusions just reached. First, Matthew cannot be said to have drawn upon Isa 61 independently of his tradition. Apart from the beatitudes and 11.5 (both from Q), there are no allusions to the chapter in his book. Which is to say: the first evangelist shows no special interest in Isa. 61. Secondly, 11.5 – Lk. 7.22 ends by clearly borrowing from Isa. 61.1 ('and good news is preached to the poor'), and this is immediately followed by a beatitude: 'And blessed is he who is not offended at me.' Now can this second association of Isa. 61.1 with a beatitude be treated as the fruit of coincidence? Probably not. 11.5-6 – Lk 7.22-3 seemingly shows us that Jesus associated the makarism form with the OT text about good news for the poor. Hence 11.5-6 – Lk 7.22-3 bolsters our claim that the influence of Isa. 61 upon the beatitudes should be located a the fount of the tradition."

[142]Davies and Allison, p. 438.

[143]Lindsey, *Jesus Rabbi & Lord*, p. 109: "Yet the Greek translator of Hebrew normally used Greek's future tense for the Hebrew imperfect and one of Greek's past tense for the Hebrew perfect. In this way the proverbial form of the Hebrew is lost in translation. There is no idea of the future. The point is that there were people in Jesus' experience who right then were trying to join

the Kingdom by just saying 'Lord, Lord.' Jesus did not accept them. Without doubt one of the reasons so many scholars have supposed that Jesus was in the habit of talking about 'inaugurating the Kingdom of God' or 'setting it up' some time in the future was due to their failure to take our Greek texts back to Hebrew where necessary. We find interpreters making the same mistake about proverbial sayings in such remarkable sayings as those we call the Beatitudes."

[144]Aaron BarAdon, Lecture at the University of Texas at Austin. Job not only rescued the poor who cried out for help, he provided help for even the stranger who may have been accused of a legal matter.

[145]Lange, p. 102: "They shall be filled, i.e., with righteousness. This promise applies neither exclusively to justification by faith, nor to final acquittal in judgment: but includes both justification, sanctification, and final acquittal, all of which, indeed, are inseparably connected with justification."

[146]Hagner, p. 92.

[147]Hagner, p. 93: "In view are not persons who are submissive, mild, and unassertive, but those who are humble in the sense of being oppressed (hence, 'have been humbled,' bent over by the injustice of the ungodly, but who are soon to realize their reward. Those in such a condition have no recourse but to depend upon God. The Qumran community revered Ps 37 and saw themselves as those about to experience the vindication that would come with messianic fulfillment (4QpPs 37). The 'earth' (thn ghn) originally referred to the land of Israel, i.e., what was promised to the Jews beginning with the Abrahamic covenant (cf.l Gen 13:15). But in the present context of messianic fulfillment is by the eschatological passages in the prophets (e.ge., Isa 65-66)."

[148]Albright and Mann, p. 46.

[149]Trapp, p. 46.

[150]Hare, p. 39: "Probably Ps. 37:11 which originally promised tenant farmers and the owners of small plots of ground that the oppression of the wicked rich would be terminated and they would gain their fair share of the soil. In Matthew's context the ambiguous terms ge (Soil? Land? Earth?) was probably understood in its broadest sense: 'The meek will come into possession of the whole inhabited earth.'"

[151]Hare, p. 39.

[152]Davies and Allison, p. 449: "Hence 5.3 and 5.5 are in synonymous parallelism. No real difference in meaning between the two is to be discerned."

[153]Davies and Allison, p. 449: "Compare Deut. 4.1. The 'meek' or 'powerless' will possess 'the earth,' they will be set over much (cf. 25.21,23). This is eschatological reversal: the world is turned upside down. 'He who humbles himself will be exalted.'"

[154]Keener, p. 168.

[155]Keener, pp. 168-69.

[156]Yeager, pp. 333-334.

[157]Lindsey, p. 109: "The beatitudes are typical Hebrew proverbs but the tense must be rendered into English as present in form so that we can see that they are proverbial... One well-known German Semitic scholar who surely should have known better developed a famous theory which held that in giving these beatitudes Jesus was talking about a pie-in-the-sky "future" Kingdom and these were the blessings he was promising one and all for that yet-to-be Kingdom of the future!

[158]Hagner, p. 93: "The beatitude seems to reflect the language of Ps 107 (LXX:106), where, after a reference to the hungry and thirsty (v5), the Psalmist writes, 'Then they cried to the Lord in their trouble, and he delivered them from their distress' (v6), and then a few verses later continues, 'For he satisfies the thirsty and the hungry

he fills with good things' (v9), where the LXX contains the same verb χορταζειν, 'to fill,' as in Matthew. This is the language of messianic fulfillment: he has filled the hungry soul with good things (cf. Ps 107:2; for a similar sense of 'thirsting' for salvation, cf. Ps. 42:1-3; 63:1). In the first instance it is God's righteousness that satisfies (cf. the 'divine passive') these hungry and thirsty souls (cf. John 6:35; Rev 7:16-17)."

[159]Bauer, p. 196.

[160]Hare, p. 39.

[161]Hare, p. 39.

[162]Hare, p. 40: "Among those who long for God to set things right are both those who themselves suffer hunger pangs and those who mourn over an inequitable distribution of goods and services that allows millions to starve on a planet capable of providing food sufficient for all. 'How best are those who hunger and thirst to see right prevail; they shall be satisfied' (NEB)."

[163]Yeager, p. 335.

[164]Trapp, p. 46.

[165]Trapp, p. 46: "The philosophers observe of the hart or hind, that being a beast thirsty by nature, when she is pursued by dogs, by reason of heat and loss of breath, her thirst is increased...And in utmost desire: so panieth the good soul after Christ, it panieth and fainteth, it hath unto his righteousness at all times."

[166]Trapp, p. 47.

[167]Trapp, p. 47.

[168]Davies and Allison, p. 451.

[169]Davies and Allison, p. 451-452.

[170]Davies and Allison, pp. 452-453: "It is worth observing that 5:6 does not congratulate those who are as a matter of fact righteous; instead it lifts up those who are hungering and thirsting for conformity to the will of God. The distinction is a matter of some remark. Righteousness,

it is implied must be ever sought, must always be a goal which lies ahead: it is never in the grasp. Recall Lk 18.9-14, the parable of the Pharisee and the tax collector – which, as Luke has it, was addressed by Jesus to 'those who trusted in themselves that they were righteous.' In this tale, the man who thinks himself righteous is in fact not, while the one who knows his own shortcoming 'went down to his house justified.' Those who hunger and thirst after righteousness are blessed, not those who think they have attained it."

[171]Bauer, p. 196.

[172]Bivin and Blizzard, p. 60: "Even the Hebrew word 'judgment' (or 'justice') can mean 'salvation.' In the same way, the verb 'judge' often means 'save.' When David is in trouble, he cries out, 'Judge me, O God'... (Psalm 43:1). The judges of the Old Testament were saviors or deliverers of the people, and not judges in the modern sense of the word...Over and over, the Prophet Isaiah uses 'judgment' as a synonym for 'salvation:' 'Therefore judgment is far from us; and righteousness does not reach us...We look for judgment, but there is none; for salvation, but it is far from us...Judgment is turned back; and righteousness stands at a distance' (Isaiah 59:9,11,14)."

CHAPTER 6

THE BEATITUDES: MATTHEW 5:7-11 AND THE

VIRTUES OF COMMUNITY PARTICIPATIONS

As the Beatitudes continue, it seems that many modern scholars interpret the text as pursuing a catalogue of virtues. Yet, as we have demonstrated, a cultural agenda is imperative for our understanding. In the case of Matthew 5:7-11, the specifics of community life in the Hebraic world of the Mediterranean come particularly into view.

Matthew 5:7

> Matthew 5:7: *Blessed are the merciful: for they shall obtain mercy.*

In grammatical and lexical terms, there is no quandary among scholars concerning the interpretation of this beatitude. The passage is simply understood as those who are merciful are also those who show mercy. Randolph Yeager argues this term by saying, "To show mercy, and to be merciful. Often in the synoptic is the plea, 'Have mercy on me (us).' Of God showing compassion in electing sinner to salvation."[173] Yeager also points out that this verse is grammatically the same as verse 5. Theologically this verse parallels in thought Galatians 6:7, which reads: *Be not deceived; God is not mocked: for whatsoever a man soweth, that shall he also reap.* As we have been establishing a Hebraic foundation for understanding the text, it is important to continue to note this Hebraic cultural agenda, which comes into play as we view the Beatitudes.

After starting with the grammatical explanation noted above, Yeager makes a dramatic shift in his approach when commenting on this verse, which is a shift made repeatedly by other New Testament scholars as well. Yeager at this point used this part of his comments to support and embrace an almost hidden agenda held among New Testament scholars, which has guided my investigation to this point. That agenda is a Hellenistic one which to this date continues to influence, incorrectly, the Jewish roots of the Biblical text in history. Hellenism cuts the historical Jesus off from his Hebraic roots, thereby placing his teachings such as the Beatitudes into a cultural setting rendering context almost completely impossible to understand. Yeager displays this point by writing:

> Pharisaic ideas of the establishment of the Messianic Kingdom were not much interested in mercy. The Irish slogan "Don't get angry; get even" ill comports with this philosophy of Jesus. The Pharisees thought of the Messianic reign as a time when judgment upon their Roman oppressors would be ruthlessly handed out. Thus we see Jesus again cutting diametrically across the thinking of the Jerusalem Establishment. His first public utterance reveals how far below the Divine standard of ethics and religion political Israel had fallen.[174]

In the above statement, Yeager misinterpreted who the Pharisees were, what they believed, and how they believed it. Addressing each of these elements in truth clarifies his probable motivation.

The first mistake is a social-historical one. Yeager undoubtedly grouped all Pharisees together, a common mistake made by many New Testament scholars. During the early first century there were several "sects" of Pharisees. There were the "Essenes," the "Zealots," and the "Hasidim" to name only three; historically there were several others among the sect of Jews. The interesting point in naming these three sects in particular centered on their distinct focus of belief, since the Hebrew word "Pharisee," is derived from the word Parush, or the Aramaic Perishaya, and carries the meaning "separate or set apart from."[175] The Essenes journeyed into the wilderness, where they formed a community and became known as the Dead Sea people. The Zealots, on the other hand, who seem to be the group Yeager refers to in the above statement, are those who looked for a messiah who would set up a political kingdom. In contrast, the Hasid, a group quite possibly unknown to Yeager, which is a distinguished sect of Israelites (Jews), were among the "Pious Men" of Israel. What Yeager set up as one group therefore has, at a minimum, three distinct motivations: one social-separatist, one political, and one more theologically driven. Moreover, each would oppose the so-called "Jerusalem establishment" in a distinct way – and not globally. The discussion of "mercy" thus needs to be revisited, if we are to understand the sense behind the passage under discussion.

In the statement above, Yeager demonstrates that he knew very little about who the Pharisees were, and what their connection was to the *Messianic kingdom,* and to *mercy.* Yeager's first mistake was to say: "Pharisaic ideas of the establishment of the Messianic Kingdom were not much interested in mercy."[176] The Hebrew word חסיד (or in English Hasid), comes from the root word חסד and is defined as, *goodness, kindness, mercy.* In connection with man it means: "*kindness* of men towards men, in doing favours and benefits...of God *kindness, loving kindness* in condescending to the needs of his creatures."[177] Hillel, the great Sage who died in the year 1, is identified as being a חסיד which according to Psalms denotes "a pious man who, in all adversity, put his trust in God."[178] Buchler writes concerning Hillel and the Hasid:

> The pious man in the other Baraitha not only avoided all sin, which in itself is only a negative virtue; but, whenever he acted, his only motive was God whose will he was thereby carrying out. And when the disciple of R. Johanan b. Zakkai, R. Joses the priest (Aboth II, 12) said, 'Let all thy deeds be done for the sake of God,' he intended to impress the highest principle to guide a man's actions: God should ever be present in his mind, and, whatever he does, whether it is great or small, important or indifferent, religious or moral, he should, like Hillel, think of God, and measure his deed by the will and honour of God; not his own benefit or pleasure, nor his own ambition and glory, but only God's honour.[179]

The above statement defined the actions displayed by one who would be considered merciful in his dealing with others and with God. To that end, the statement by Yeager that Pharisees were not interested in mercy because of their eschatological perspective on the Messianic Kingdom is totally incorrect. In terms of God's honor "measuring deeds" calls for an individual not to judge others, nor to take the role of God unto one's self.

The second statement Yeager used in his comments concerning the meaning of mercy was: "the Pharisees thought of the Messianic reign as a time when judgment upon their Roman oppressors would be ruthlessly handed out." This statement by Yeager is misleading and anti-Jewish in nature. Instead of recognizing the diversity among Jewish sects, Yeager placed the hatred of the Roman oppressors fully on the shoulders of the Pharisees, creating the impression that such resistance was general. Yet historically, it was the Jewish Zealots who took this position against the Roman Empire aggressively. In a book by David Flusser, *Jesus*, he writes concerning the zealots:

> At that time most Jews hated the occupying Roman power. The party known as the Zealots believed that armed struggle against Rome was divinely ordained, and their terrorist activists made the country unsafe. One of the twelve apostles had been a Zealot at one time. The fundamental teaching of the Zealots was "the demand for the sole rule of God," which led to a radical breach with the Roman Caesar's claims to sovereignty. It was linked with the expectation that, through battle with the Roman oppressor, the eschatological liberation of Israel at the end of time would be ushered in. Although it is possible that the Zealots, too, spoke about the kingdom of heaven, at that time the phrase had in fact become an anti-Zealot slogan. Because there are clear similarities between the rabbinic idea of the kingdom and that of Jesus, we may assume that Jesus developed their idea. This concept did not appear among the Essenes.[180]

According to Flusser, the Zealots were indeed in full support of being liberated from under the yoke of Rome, in a natural sense and in a spiritual sense – but the Essenes were not necessarily concerned with that separation. Stressing how very political (anti-imperial) the Zealots were, he also states: "A Zealot is not likely to have had much sympathy for the crucified, nonpolitical, suffering Messiah."[181] That is, they believed the political Messianic Kingdom of Heaven inaugurated by Jesus had nothing to do with setting up the Davidic kingdom of David.

Flusser further clarifies the position by Yeager and other scholars which confuses a political and a theological community, when he states:

> We have indicated that in Judaism the coming of an eschatological Redeemer and the kingdom of heaven are two different structures. So it was in Jesus' mind. This explains why Jesus did not try to bring these two independent systems into a complete harmony. He recognized that the kingdom of heaven is a dynamic power with an imminent tendency to spread on earth, but he did not say (nor did he probably believe) that the final realization of the kingdom of heaven would culminate with the coming of the Son of Man and the Last Judgment...When the centrality of the Messiah increased, however, the conception of the messianic era emerged. It created a tendency to insert this era into the current eschatological scheme. The solutions were not simply a compromise, as is often thought today. The only possibility was to let the messianic era follow our historical period, placing the Day of the Messiah prior to the post-historical period, "the age to come." In so doing, a clear division between history and "post-history" was finally achieved. "The Days of the Messiah" belong, strictly speaking, to the

history of mankind, while the "age to come" is considered beyond current history.[182]

In the above statement, Flusser establishes that there are two distinct messianic periods, two different sets of goals implied by the reports of Jesus' actions, one theological and one more political-practical. The first is represented as the age to come, in which the Messiah or the *Ha Ba* inaugurates the Kingdom of Heaven as a spiritual rule of God. This spiritual period, according to Jesus is at hand (Luke 10:9).

The *Ha Ba* or *Bar Enash* ('the coming one or the Son of Man') was known as the Messiah of Daniel 7:13-14. The text reads:

> *In my vision at night I looked, and there before me was one like a Son of Man, coming with the clouds of heaven. He approached the Ancient of Days and was led into his presence. He was given authority, glory and sovereign power; all people, nations and men of every language worshiped him, His dominion is an everlasting dominion that will not pass away, and his kingdom is one that will never be destroyed.* (NIV)

This passage makes a proclamation of the coming Messiah who will be known as "The Son of Man," and further distinguishes the purpose of this kingdom by setting the stage on which those who studied the text would recognize the coming Messiah or Son of Man.

One last point about Yeager and verse 7. He also said the "first public utterance reveals how far below the Divine standard of ethics and religion political Israel had fallen," which in and of itself is another totally misrepresented phrase. In light of the history of the first century, scholars like Yeager overlooked evidence that clearly support a different reality during this time. In the book *Our Father Abraham*, Marvin Wilson writes:

> In Romans 9-11, Paul discusses the present and future of Jew and Gentile in the plan of God. His stress on justification by faith rather than the works of the Law leads some scholars to argue that Paul sees the Jew and Torah permanently set aside. But the apostle himself says, "By no means!" (Rom. 11:1). As Krister Stendahl rightly points out, "Romans 9-11 is not an appendix to chapters 1-8, but the climax of the letter." In Romans 11, Paul warns those who have come to faith out of gentile backgrounds not to "boast" (v. 18) or become "arrogant" (v. 20). They are but wild olive branches grafted into the olive tree (Israel, v. 24), allowed by God's goodness to "share in the nourishing sap from the olive root" (v. 17). Here Paul points to a unity between Israel (the tree) and the Gentiles (the in grafted branches) by drawing upon a horticultural metaphor familiar from the Old Testament. It is Hebraic through and through. Of Israel Jeremiah writes, "The Lord called you a thriving olive tree, with fruit beautiful in form" (Jer. 11:16). Also concerning Israel Hosea states, "His splendor will be like an olive tree" (Hos. 14:6).[183]

Biblical evidence does not support the claim that Israel had fallen in its Divine ethics and in its religion. Yeager's statement concerning Israel was clearly an intentional misdirection, turning a political statement (the specific political goal of the Zealots) into a generalized comment on theology, one that ignores how very vibrant the specifically Hebraic theological arguments of the era were and still are.

Returning to the philology of the passage helps to confirm this assertion in its own way. In the second half of verse 7, the merciful, *they obtain mercy,* is supported in the commentaries of each scholar's work. However, the Hebrew word in verse 7 that most translators translate as *mercy* is the word ירחמו which comes from the root word רחם and is defined as *compassion, compassionate.*[184] To illustrate in another way the meaning of רחם, we can turn to Isaiah 60:10 for a final confirmation, which says: *Foreigners will rebuild your walls, and their kings will serve you. Though in anger I struck you, in favor I will show you compassion.*

Here, then, is a less moralistic version of the term "mercy," one that takes it meaning as a political statement referring to empire, not just as a personal-psychological trait. In Proverbs 28:13 (*He who covers his transgressions will not prosper. But whoever confesses and forsakes his sins, shall obtain mercy*), the one who confesses his sins and forsakes his sins is the one who obtains mercy. Thus to obtain mercy means to obtain forgiveness; therefore, he who shows compassion in forgiving will also obtain forgiveness.

A contemporary Hebraic translation of Matthew 5:7 might better read: *Blessed are those who are forgiving, for they shall be forgiven.*

Matthew 5:8

Matthew 5:8: *Blessed are the pure in heart: for they shall see God.*

As the Beatitudes go on, this tension between the psychological elements of theology seen from the Hellenistic context and from the Hebraic one continues. Some scholars are beginning to reclaim the true meaning of the text as they consider these verses more directly within the Hebraic context. Albright and Mann opened their interpretation of this verse by saying a *pure-mind* is spiritually equivalent to being ritually pure. They also supported the belief that *pure* is best represented by the Aramaic word *dakhin*, "broken, humble, contrite." Concerning the issue of a pure heart, Albright and Mann write:

> The theme of purity of heart is well attested in rabbinic literature; cf. "The Holy One, blessed be He, loves everyone who is pure of heart" (Midrash *Rabba* on Gen Xl 8), or "R. Jose ben Halafta said to R. Ishmael his son, 'If you seek to see the face of the Shekinah' – i.e., the abiding presence of God – in this world, study the Torah in the land of Israel'" (Midrash *Shokker Tob* on Ps cv). (Both references by the kindness of Dr. Aberbach).[185]

This statement places the phrase 'pure in heart' back into its Hebraic setting. Apart from their reference to Aramaic as the original language of the passage, Albright and Mann's juxtaposition of these Hebrew sources clearly provides the reader with a better understanding of this verse.

Samuel Tobias Lachs, in *A Rabbinic Commentary on the New Testament*, augers that Isaiah 61:1 best represents the Hebraic sense of this verse. Lachs provides a transliteration of the Hebrew with these words, noting the 'pure in heart,' *bar lev*, goes back to *nishbare lev* of Isaiah 61:1. He summarizes by calling this a "haplography of the first two words, *asher [nish] bare lev*, what remained was *ashre bare lev*, 'blessed are the pure in heart.'"[186] He also states that *for they shall see God* is actually a madras on the text *v'la'asurim peqah qo'ah*, also from Isaiah 61:1. To see God, according to Lachs, is an expression found in rabbinic sources meaning, "to see the Shekhinah" and "is employed as a reward for the performance of a meritorious act."[187] Lachs points out that "the use of Shekhinah as a reward for the performance of a *mizvah*" is common. However, because of the nature of his statement, it is worth quoting his argument at length:

> R. Dostai b. Jannai expounded: 'Observe that the ways of God are not like the ways of flesh and blood. How does flesh and blood act? If a man brings a present to a king, it may be accepted or it may not be accepted, even if it is accepted it is still doubtful whether he will be admitted to the presence of the king or not. Not so with God. If a man gives a coin to a beggar he is deemed worthy to receive the Divine Presence, as it is written, *I shall behold Thy face in righteousness, I shall be satisfied when I awake with Thy likeness* [Ps 17.15].'

> R. Menashah the grandson of R. Joshua b. Levi said: 'We find that if a person happens to see a naked part of the body and does not feed his eyes upon it, he is worthy of given welcome to the Shekhina. What is his reason? It says, *and shut his eyes from looking upon evil* [Isa. 33.15]. What is written after this? *Thine eyes shall see the king in His beauty, they shall behold a land stretching afar.*'

> R. Simeon b. Yohhai says: 'Whoever is scrupulous in the observance of this *mizvah* is worthy to receive the Divine Presence, for it is written, *that you may look upon it* [Num. 14.39], and it is written *thou shalt fear the Lord thy God, Him shalt thou serve* [Deut. 6.14].'[188]

In the above statement, Lachs finds an interpretation of the Shekhinah as the center of where life comes from.

Thus accordingly acts of mercy are worthy of the Shekhinah that dwells within them. Lachs also points out that the word Shekhinah "is not simply a substitute for the Divine Name but most often used as a technical term of God's immanence."[189] Wherein, "God's immanence" is an excellent way to show that a theological argument from rabbinic literature could indeed have had political weight at the time, and that, in turn, acknowledging the politics of the argument does not destroy the theological validity it had in the era.

Donald Hagner's commentary on this passage, however, is one who confirms the doubled sense of the Beatitudes here, while denying its politics. He correctly parallels verse 7 with that of Psalms 24:3-4, which reads: *Who may ascend the hill of the Lord? Who may stand in his holy place? He who has clean hands and a pure heart, who does not lift up his soul to an idol or swear by what is false* (NIV). Yet according to Hagner, "pure in heart" "refers to the condition of the inner core of a person, that is, thoughts and motivation, and hence anticipates the internalizing of the commandments by Jesus in the material that follows in the sermon."[190] Hagner says that the expression "seeing God" is a hint to the eschatological coming kingdom. Thereby, those who have guiltless hands will receive the reward in the coming kingdom, the privilege of seeing God face to face. He further suggests that the downtrodden, the oppressed, would be rewarded because of their inner purity – a condition not necessarily related to other life concerns. Not surprisingly, he closed by saying that this Beatitude did not relate to the others – a conclusion I must refute. Hagner by placing his comments on guiltless hands will receive a reward to see God face to face. This allowed him to draw upon strong emotions by interpreting this passage with what I call "Sounds good Theology," an interpretation which voids the spiritual values taught by Jesus in this Beatitude.

That error stems from commentators' continued reluctance to deal with these passages in a comprehensive context. Taking the opposite tactic, by concluding and ending at the same place, a Hellenistic perspective, Douglas Hare opened his commentary on verse 8 and takes the position that "the Greek adjective *kitharas* means both clean, as in "a clean linen shroud" (Matt. 27:59), and pure, that is, unadulterated or unalloyed, as in "pure gold" (Rev. 21:21).[191] Hare also felt that the parallel of Psalms 24:4 "clean hands" and "pure hands" was an indication that those who were of a "pure heart" were also those who were innocent of moral failures, and evil intentions. He quotes Romans 3:23 to support this position, but then he turns by reflecting his personal confusion in these words:

> Either the psalmist is unduly optimistic about the perfectibility of the saints or he is using the term to designate something other than absolute moral perfection. Perhaps he means those who are innocent regarding the grosser sins (murder, adultery, theft). On the other hand, perhaps he is using the adjective in its other sense, "unalloyed." The same Hebrew root occurs in this sense in II Sam. 22:27: "With the pure thou dost show thyself pure," where there is no question of God being immoral when dealing with the immoral. Taken in this way, the pure in heart are those whose devotion to God is unalloyed. They are not double minded (James 1:8); they do not attempt to serve both mammon and God (Matt. 6:24). Such an understanding accords well with the thesis enunciated by Kierkegaard in his book, *Purity of Heart is to Will One Thing*.[192]

For Hare, the phrase "pure in heart" begins to take on a sense of perfection, not just in conduct but also in moral behaviors that could only be displayed in a sinful life. His confusion seems to center around the word "unalloyed" as a description of a moral and spiritual life – he cannot see that the two are reconcilable, as they are not from a Hellenistic point of view, but they were in the Hebraic worlds. To support his point of view, Hare used the passages found in II Samuel 22:27, which speak of God as not being immoral when dealing with those who are immoral. Had Hare read the passages just above verse 27 in Samuel, he might not have suggested this text as support for his interpretation of Matthew 5:8. The text in II Samuel 22:21-28 reads:

> The Lord has dealt with me according to my righteousness; according to the cleanness of my hands he has rewarded me. For I have kept the ways of the Lord; I have not done evil by turning from my God. All his laws are before me; I have not turned away from his decrees. I have been blameless before him and have kept myself from sin. The Lord has rewarded me according to my righteousness, according to my cleanness in his sight. To the faithful you show yourself faithful, but to the crooked you show yourself shrewd. You save the humble, but your eyes are on the haughty to bring them low. (NIV)

Hare used the word "unalloyed" to indicate his understanding that those who are pure in heart, and have reached some type of unmixed status in their human behavior – some unity in soul, manifested it in outward behavior. However, the text in II Samuel 22:21-28 does not address conduct or moral status, nor is it referring to a state of perfection in life. It does establish the condition in which II Samuel 22:7 should be interpreted with "cleanliness" referring to both statuses at once. Reward me according to my righteousness, thus, accordingly pure in heart is compared to that of righteousness in deeds. Hare is thus at pains to restrict the reading to a discourse of abstract virtues, while the text is addressing conduct, the way a believer lives in the sight of God.

Yet II Samuel 22:21 is also one of the keys in understanding how verse 27 should be interpreted, taking into account the practical side of the abstract moral dictum. The word "righteousness" from the Hebrew text carries the meaning of *acts of loving kindness, God's righteous judgment, God's redeeming power*, which is an attribute of God displayed in those who are pure in heart. Just like God, they too are charged to display acts of loving kindness in their dealings on the earth, especially with those who are downtrodden. In natural conditions of life (not just as a state of soul) the pure in heart are those innocent in their dealings with others, and thereby those whose actions produce clean hands, not a virtue based upon one's justification.

Here again, opening our eyes to the more literal, realistic, social-political references to the verses clarifies their sense. In the reading of Matthew 5:8, *Blessed are those who are pure in heart*, it deals with those who are blameless more than it does with those who are prefect. They are "blameless" in that they have not lifted up unclean hands before God – hands that have not become unclean in their dealing with their fellow man. The expression "pure in heart" can also be clarified in the same way, as defining those who deal justly with those in need. The pure in heart provide redemption, deliverance, vindication, and salvation to those hurting and in need; any actions counter to these would necessarily be understood as the opposite of *pure in heart*.

However, in the context of Psalms 24:4 and Matthew 5:8, it means never to have lifted yourself up to falsehood nor to have sworn deceitfully; thus this is the one who has clean hands and a pure heart. One of the Ten Commandments (Exodus 20:16), *Thou shalt not bear false witness against*

155

thy neighbor, also deals with the court of law where testimonies are rendered. When a person is on trial for his life (Numbers 35:30) it is the testimony of at least two witnesses that makes a judgment final (Deut. 19:15), while the false testimony of one person is not enough to put a man to death. The last part of verse 8, *they shall see God*, amplifies this distinction, since it speaks not to the eschatological coming kingdom, in which the pure in heart shall take pleasure in seeing God face to face. Instead, it might be possible that, according to the Semitic concept underlying this text, it points more toward the spiritual benefit of displaying the attribute of being pure in heart on earth, thereby becoming one with God's nature. In this case, God's attribute can be seen on earth when displayed by those possessing this God-like characteristic.

A contemporary Hebraic translation of Matthew 5:8 might thus read: *Happy are those who have never lifted themselves up to falsehood to intentionally deceive. Happy are those who are people of integrity, for they shall see God, God's attributes, God's nature.* That is, they see the God-principle in all who contribute to the well being of the group.

Matthew 5:9

> Matthew 5:9: *Blessed are the peacemakers: for they shall be called the children of God.*

The question of "peacemaking" takes up the comparison between a good life and more abstract categories in another way. Albright and Mann begin their commentary on verse 9 by making several textual comparisons. Referring to the Qmt source, Albright and Mann write:

> This verse linked up, on verbal and thematic grounds, with 5:38-48 – Lk 6:27-30, 32-6 (on

turning the other cheek and loving enemies). In its present context in Matthew the verse is also nicely illustrated by 5:21-6 (on setting aside anger and making friends with enemies).[193]

For Albright and Mann, this beatitude takes on the meaning of turning the other cheek and loving your enemies. They further their interpretation by saying:

Μακαριοι οι ειρηνοποιοι. Compare 2 En. 52.11-15. 'Peacemaker,' not 'pacifist' or 'peaceful,' is the right translation of ειρηνοποιπξ for a positive action, reconciliation, is envisioned; the 'peacemakers' seek to bring about peace (see Dupont 3, pp. 635-640). The word is a LXX and NT *hapax legomenon,* and the theme of 'peace' is not prominent in the first Gospel. Both of these facts supply evidence for a pre-Matthean origin. The verbal equivalent of 'peacemaker' occurs in Prov 10.10 LXX ('He who boldly reproves makes peace') and Col. 1.20. Compare Jas. 3.18: 'The harvest of righteousness is sown in peace by those who make peace'...Because there is no qualification for 'peacemakers,' it would be wrong to delimit precisely the sphere to which the 'peacemakers' bring peace (see Schnackenburg (v)), although in view of the consistent social dimension in the texts just quoted above, religious peace ('peace with God') is probably not the subject. (Origen's inclusion of those who reconcile contradictory Biblical texts among the 'peacemakers' (*Philocal.* 6.1) is only a curiosity which evokes a smile.) Perhaps our beatitude was first formulated during the Jewish war or shortly thereafter and reflects the conviction that revolution against Rome was the wrong course to take...In being a peacemaker, the disciple is imitating his Father in heaven, 'the God of peace' (Rom 16.20, cf. T. Dan. 5.2; Rom 15.33; Phil 4.9; I Th 5.23; 2 Th 3.16; Heb 13.20)[194]

In this statement, the term "peacemaker" again refers to a real situation faced by communities, not only to abstract values. It takes as its basis a war-like perspective, wherein those who are peacemakers are they who take on the position of peace.

Albright and Mann cite more than twenty passages to illustrate their interpretation of what a peacemaker is in verse 9, using a Rabbinic text from *Aboth* 1:12 to also support their position. Nonetheless, in paralleling and contrasting various usages of this term, they still fall far short of its biblical meaning because they do not bring larger community concerns to the fore in ways that would echo for contemporaneous readers. They again ignore the historical subtleties about which groups actually were espousing war at the time.

In the commentary by Randolph Yeager, the peacemaker continues to be defined as the opposite to those who make war, an assumption that reveals why this distinction is overly simplistic. Yeager takes this opportunity to attribute to the Pharisees yet another non-historically attested attitude. He states that "the peacemakers, not the patriotic warmongers like the jingoistic Pharisees – they and none other, the sons of God, will be called."[195] Again trying clearly to distance his view of Jesus from the details of the historical situation. Yeager concludes this part of his commentary with these interesting words:

As has already been suggested, the first seven Beatitudes set forth a sevenfold perfection of Christian character, with an accompanying seven-fold blessedness. The experience of a sinner receiving salvation is also seen in the same sequence. First he becomes humble in spirit – an intellectual acceptance of his spiritual poverty (vs. 3); then he mourns (vs. 4) the emotional reaction; meekness (vs. 5) follows and is followed by a hunger and thirst for righteousness (vs. 6), which longing is satisfied and the sinner is saved. Three fruitages appear as immediate results of his new-found salvation: He becomes merciful (vs. 7) and thus obtains mercy; he has purity of heart and begins to understand God as he grows in grace and in the knowledge of Christ (vs. 8) and becomes a maker of peace and thus commends himself to the world as a child of God.[196]

In this statement Yeager's theological rendering of the Beatitudes is quite interesting and makes for a good homily from the Christian-Hellenized point of view, stressing values. Again, Yeager's statement above can be defined as a type of "Sounds good Theology," where religious terms or concepts are used that sound good but mean absolutely nothing to a precise unfolding of textual meaning.

The peacemaker, in Douglas Hare's commentary does not fare much better since this interpreter takes the same approach as his colleagues. In his reading, peacemakers are not persons living in peace under the fruits of protection. They are in contrast "those who devote themselves to the hard work of reconciling hostile individuals, families, groups, and nations."[197] To show what is lacking, one need only follow Hare's method in justifying his conclusion. Hare's interpretation of this passage, for instance, refers to the Hebrew word *Shalom* (peace), but failed to use the Hebrew lexicon definition of this word *Shalom*. Instead, *peace* as it is defined in English became a weak and incomplete synonym for the Hebrew word *Shalom*. According to Hare:

The creators of *shalom* will deserve to be called the sons and daughter of God, because they have chosen to imitate his magnanimity. Remembering that he makes his sun rise on the evil and on the good, and sends rain on the just and on the unjust (Matt. 5:45), they strive to return good for evil and to love those they do not like. Where others build walls, they painstakingly construct bridges. The efforts of peacemakers often seem utterly futile, but their work is never unsuccessful. Their living testimony to God's intended *shalom* keeps the vision alive.[198]

This sounds compelling to today's ear, but it is an incomplete account. In *The Hebrew-English Lexicon* by Brown-Driver-Briggs, the word *Shalom* is defined as, *completeness, soundness, welfare, wholeness, prosperity, safety*, and *peace*. It is clear that the original statement defined a peacemaker as a type of diplomat whose focus is to keep the peace between nations or individuals. This is thus not only a spiritual state, but, one of an active community and national effort.

Another recent approach to this passage that provides an extended definition are the words of Marvin Wilson, who writes concerning the word peace (Shalom).

Many homes today are marked by internal strife, conflict, and tension. Too often they have become battlegrounds where quarrels and disputes break forth daily. The ancient rabbis warned about the danger of bickering and controversy within the home: 'Anger in the home is like worms in grain' (Babylonian Talmud, Sotah 3b), 'A home where there is dissension will not stand' (Derekh Eretz Zuta 9:12 [a section of one of the minor tractates in the Talmud.]). The apostle Paul likewise cautioned about how lack of harmony brings sure destruction: "The entire law is summed up in a single command: 'Love your neighbor as yourself.' If you keep on biting and devouring each other, watch out or you will be destroyed by each other." (Gal. 5:14-15) The Hebrew Scriptures command, however, that the people of God must "seek peace and pursue it" (Ps. 34:14b). In Judaism, therefore, one of the most important family values is that of *shalom bayit*, "a peaceful home." In the presence of strangers or among casual acquaintances in the community, it is usually not too difficult to pass the test of *shalom*. But *shalom* is difficult to maintain in the home. There the true mettle of one's character is tested on a day-to-day basis. It is in the home that tempers can flare up at the smallest provocation. Accordingly, the Talmud insists that conversation with people be "gentle." (Yoma 86a)[199]

Wilson sets the tone for understanding a peacemaker in verse 9, by referring to the natural pressures individuals experience day-to-day in their homes. A peacemaker has to be able to live in a state of mind in peace, and yet be the peacemaker among those he loves the most – the peacemaker is a moral and a community force. Wilson then goes on to introduce his reader to an amplified concept of *shalom bayit* (a peaceful home), and says that this term is one of the most important concepts in Judaism. He writes:

A home of *shalom*, therefore, is a healthy home. Strife brings sickness, but *shalom* is wellness and wholeness. Strife divides, but *shalom* unites. Jesus taught, "Blessed are the peacemakers" (Matt. 5:9). Paul says that peace is the fruit of the Spirit within

(Gal. 5:22). Here lies the Christian's key to *shalom bayit*, "a peaceful home." Shalom is supernaturally produced in the life of each believer. The unity of the home, and of all God's people, is the unity of the Spirit (cf. Eph. 4:3).[200]

For the purposes of the present argument, it is important to note that Wilson is absolutely correct in paralleling the human suffering condition with that of the duties of a peacemaker. The peacemakers, according to Matthew 5:9, are those who are bringing others who are suffering into *wholeness, soundness, completeness*, those who are especially bringing healing in the household of those hurting to overcome strife. God is referred to as a peacemaker in Job 25:2. In Jewish sources Aaron is believed to have been a peacemaker in Numbers 6:23-36. Brad Young addresses the meaning of a peacemaker, as he writes:

> Aaron and his followers pursued peace. As priests they were mediators not only between God and his people but also between individuals who had broken relationships. According to the rabbis, the priests tried to heal family wounds. They restored peace between a disputing husband and wife. We know this from an early rabbinic text, Avot deRabbi Nathan, which adds the qualification to the saying of Hillel, "Be of the disciples of Aaron, loving peace and pursuing peace, *promoting peace between man and wife.*" In other words, the rabbis viewed Hillel's remarks as promoting peace in the family. Aaron and his disciples mediated the disputes. Husband and wives must live in peace one with the other.[201]

There is one further analogy to be made about the term in this passage. In Lachs' commentary, he points out that the term "peacemakers," however, are nowhere in rabbinic literature called 'the children of God.' Hillel called peacemakers 'disciples of Aaron.' Hillel said: "Be of the disciples of Aaron, loving peace, and pursuing peace, loving your fellow creatures and bringing them near to the Torah."[202]

A contemporary Hebraic translation of Matthew 5:9 might therefore read: *Happy are those who are bringing men and women into wholeness, into completeness, into salvation; these are those who are called Sons of the Living God.*

These three verses from Matthew cluster very tightly around notions of community. Reaching back to the general cultural setting in which the Beatitudes are introduced – as passages for the individual teaching rabbi to expand on – it is clear that each has two faces. The first is that adduced by the majority of commentators: these passages discuss general social and personal virtues – peace, mercy, and purity. Yet in adding information from the historical setting to our readings of these passages, clear social and political implications emerge and are addressed. They take active positions on how the community was to relate to Roman-era politics, to their families and peers, and to their communities as a whole. Each, accordingly, could be traced even further, to correlate with the specific positions taken by various Pharisee groups in each of these contexts – a project beyond the scope of the present discussion.

However, the Beatitudes also present implications for more than individual virtues or for the community, as we shall see in the next chapter of this discussion. They contain more active political materials, as well.

NOTES FOR CHAPTER 6

[173]Yeager, p. 336: "Of a Christian's attempt to win the lost –
Jude 22,23. To show mercy to a sick man – Phil. 2:27."

[174]Yeager, p. 336: "The reason why the child of God should
be merciful is simple. Judgment is reserved only to
the One who died for our sins to rescue us from their
horrible results. Since no man can pay the sinner's sin
debt and rescue him, no man has the right to judge him
for his sins. John 5:22."

[175]See my article "Characteristics of Pharisees," www.
wmcdonaldministry.com. "The Greek language sources
(particularly Josephus and the N.T.) refer to *perishaya* as
pharisaioi. The Semitic language sources (particularly
rabbinic sources) refer to the *parush* as *perushim*. This
concept of being separated, according to the rabbis, can
be seen in the books of Ezra, as it speaks of those who
returned from the Babylonia Exile. They had *parush*/
separated themselves from the filthiness of the nations
of the land (Ezra 6:21)."

[176]Yeager, p. 336.

[177]Brown-Driver-Briggs, pp. 338-339.

[178]Adolph Buchler, *Types of Jewish-Palestinian Piety: From 70 B.C.E. To 70 C.E. The Ancient Pious Men* (New York: Ktav Publishing House, Inc. 1922) p. 7.

[179]Buchler, p. 18: "An instructive instance of Hillel's way of thinking and of his religious reflection on ordinary actions of his has fortunately been preserved. When once Hillel had taken leave of his disciple (in the school), he went with them; to their question as to where he was going, he replied, 'To perform a religious duty;' and this he explained to mean bathing in a public bath. To their further question as to whether that was a religious duty, he said, 'The man appointed to the duty of scouring and rinsing the statues of the King set up in the theatres and circuses is for that paid by maintenance, and, in addition, he is one of the government officials. As I was created in the image and after the likeness (of God), as it says (Gen. 9:6), 'for in the image of God made He man:' how much more so (have I to wash my body).' It need hardly be pointed out that a man with that conception of his body – for to this and not to the soul does the image of God here refer – ever present in his mind, kept his body clean not only physically, but also morally, free from any kind of pollution; and even his physical use of it for natural functions, as at easing it or in sexual intercourse, was hallowed, even though he was not an Essene." p. 19.

[180]Flusser, pp. 105-106.

[181]Flusser, p. 227: "As with the crowd of the Jewish people who are sympathetic to the crucified one, the mocking enemies of Jesus also correspond to historical probability in Luke. 'The rulers' (archontes) is Luke's name for the dignitaries who delivered Jesus up to the Romans, and the mockery of the Roman soldiers is natural.

According to Luke, Jesus is only derided by one of the malefactors crucified with him, but according to Mark and Matthew he is mocked by both. In this case they are either criminals or, more likely, zealots from the group around Barabbas."

[182]Flusser, pp. 268-269.

[183]Wilson, pp. 114-115.

[184]Brown-Driver-Briggs. p. 933.

[185]Albright and Mann, p. 47.

[186]Samuel Tobias Lachs, *A Rabbinic Commentary on the New Testament: The Gospels of Matthew, Mark, and Luke* (Hoboken, New Jersey: KTAV Publishing House, Inc. 1946) p. 74.

[187]Lachs, p. 76: "He who does such-and-so is worthy that the Shekhinah dwell with him. Shekhinah is not simply a substitute term for the Divine Name but most often used as a technical term of God's immanence."

[188]Lachs, p. 76.

[189]Lachs, p. 76.

[190]Hagner, p. 94: "It takes for granted right actions but asks for integrity in the doing of those actions, i.e., a consistency between the inner springs of one's conduct and the conduct itself. Another way of putting this is in terms of 'single-mindedness' (cf. Jas. 4:8, where it is the 'double-minded' who are exhorted to 'purify [their] hearts'). Purity of heart and purity of conscience are closely related in the pastoral Epistles (cf. I Tim. 1:5; 3:9; 2 Tim 1:3; 2:22; cf. I Pet 1:22)."

[191]Hare, p. 41.

[192]Hare, p. 41.

[193]Albright and Mann, p. 457.

[194]Albright and Mann. p. 457-458.

[195]Yeager, p. 340: "What they are called – 'sons of God' is emphasized over the fact that they will be so called. Thus God, who is a God of peace, because He alone

knows the answer to man's sin and rebellion, which is the cause of war, is in the process of bringing many sons into glory, who, because, being pure in heart and thus peacemakers, demonstrate the characteristics of their Father. Like Father, like Sons."

[196]Yeager, p. 340.

[197]Hare, p. 42: "It is noteworthy that the beatitude was first uttered during the Pax Romana. By dint of military superiority the Romans had put an end to small wars between competing client states, had rid the Mediterranean Sea of pirates, and had greatly diminished brigandage on land."

[198]Hare, p. 42.

[199]Wilson, pp. 217-218.

[200]Wilson, p. 218: "Paul warns fathers, 'do not exasperate your children' (Eph. 6:4). Rather than provoking their offspring to anger, fathers are to be a sensitive model of maturity and stability and peace before their children. Indeed, Paul exhorts all believers to 'live in harmony with one another' (Rom. 12:16). Harmony is destroyed by the acts of the sinful nature, which include hatred, discord, jealousy, fits of rage, selfish ambition, dissensions, factions, and envy, and 'those who live like this will not inherit the kingdom of God' (see Gal. 5:19-21)."

[201]Young, *Jesus And His Jewish Parables*, p. 87: "The Hebrew word for peace, Shalom, however, has a much greater range of meanings. It is derived from the three-letter root *sh-l-m* (שׁ ל מ) which means 'to make complete or whole.' In the Bible when someone inquires concerning another person's well-being, he or she simply asks, 'How is your peace?' The word refers to a person's health, spiritual state, or even his or her prosperity. In essence it includes every aspect of an individual's well-being and inner strength. Peace in Hebrew means wholeness or completeness. In certain ways it denotes a person's

healing or salvation. Someone who is saved from life's difficulties experiences the peace of God through the wholeness which comes by divine grace and favor."

[202]Lachs, p. 76: "The peacemaker is, however, called blessed: 'Blessed is he who established peace and love. Blessed is he who goes [sc. One that has] and brings [sc. Other] together in peace.' 'Cursed is he who disturbs what is in peace. Blessed is he who speaks peace and has peace.'"

CHAPTER 7

THE BEATITUDE OF PERSECUTION

Matthew 5:10

Matthew 5:10: *Blessed are they which are persecuted for righteousness sake: for theirs is the kingdom of heaven.*

Donald Hagner takes the position that persecution, the theme of this beatitude, is important in Matthew, a theme that reflects those to whom the Gospels were written. Again in the tradition of Hellenistic scholars, Hagner takes the position that this passage is addressed to those who would be persecuted, namely the Jewish brethren. He also used this presumed ongoing persecution of the early Jewish Christian as the reason why Jesus taught his followers how to endure a state of being. For him, the poor in spirit of verse 3 are the same as the persecuted in verse 10, because they both inherit the Kingdom of Heaven. Such a parallel fits the image of the emerging Christian church as the church of martyrs, a new martyrdom growing out of the Jew's tradition of oppression within the growing Roman Empire.

Hagner further embraces this image of Jews as showing a suffering servant spirit when he states that it was "an honored tradition they stand in when they suffered persecution."[203] In this way, he cross-referenced suffering of the righteous at the hands of their persecutors with Jewish history as a supposedly natural part of the history of Israel. Following a similar chain of association, John Lange's commentary makes an interesting (and equally incomplete or incorrect) comment on the second part of verse 10, *Theirs is the kingdom of heaven*, noting that this expression is the same as verse 3. Nevertheless, according to Lange, the reward for those who are poor in spirit, as stated in verse 3, was to be "comforted." And yet he goes one step further, assuming that those who are persecuted for righteousness will partake of the "great reward in heaven itself which is promised to all who suffer for the sake of Christ."[204] Here again, the word *heaven* is devoid completely from its historical setting. But according to Hagner and Lange the concept *heaven* embraced a particular type of Christian theology which has intruded itself into the interpretation of this passage, which has its own dynamics.

The first set of correctives to this Hellenized perspective comes quite naturally from philology itself. In the commentary work of Albright and Mann they simply concluded that this passage should be interpreted with the word *inclusio*. According to them, "this statement concludes one group of sayings, for the phrase *theirs is the Kingdom of heaven* began the series and now ends it. This device (called inclusio) is common in Matthew."[205] Thus they are interested more in showing the coherence of the set of passages as a textual unit, recognizing (most probably) that such passages were meant to be memory prompts, shorthand forms of what would have been longer complete sermons or teaching passages. From that perspective, it becomes particularly questionable to take the sense of a passage completely on the basis of how such abbreviations are worded, since the passages were not meant to stand on their own. Albright's and Mann's position clearly changes from the text being a unit to them later standing on their own. Historically and culturally Albright and Mann, Hagner and Lange, do not understand the Hebraic mind set from which these passages originated.

However, most scholars persist in taking such passages at their wording. For example, Davies and Allison began their comments on verse 10 with an exegetical analysis of this text. Their argument adopts a philological approach, suggesting a type of evidence to broaden the purely Hellenistic reading of the passage and to take more historical perspectives into account. They conclude, because there is no evidence for this passage in the Q source and no counterpart of this verse in Luke, Matthew added 5:10 to the beatitudes. Their reason for making the above statement was:

> Not in order to gain a beatitude about persecution. 5.11-12 satisfies that requirement. Nor in order to give 'righteousness' a home in the beatitudes, for it has already been named in 5.6. Nor even to connect persecution and righteousness, for the evangelist could easily have added 'and righteousness' at the end of 5.11. No, the explanation for 5.10 lies not in its content but instead in a formal consideration: without it there would be only eight beatitudes. Our evangelist has carefully arranged his material throughout chapters 5-7 so as to generate numerous triadic groupings: the number three is the key to the structure of the sermon on the mount. But if so, then the addition of 5.10 makes excellent sense. Matthew wanted the number of the beatitudes to be a multiple of three. So, having received eight beatitudes, he created one more.[206]

It is possible that the above statement is more theological than exegetical, and that it is more influenced by their own presumptions about how the text worked in its context rather than by the kinds of historical, social, and political references already argued. However, given the position Davies and Allison hold in the academic circles, the above statement has been taken as exegetical.

Be that as it may, this statement leaves important questions very much unanswered. Such as, if the evangelist inserted 5:10 to establish the beatitudes in multiples of three, it is important to ask if verse 10 does indeed represent the original words of Jesus, and his teachings to his disciples in verses 1 and 2? That assumption seems to directly contradict what we know about rabbinic teaching practices. As Davies and Allison continue, they follow the path of greater assumptions, with the statement there are no comparable passage(s) in the Old Testament addressing the blessing of the persecuted. In the commentary of Douglas Hare they argued that the key in understanding verse 10a is the word *righteousness*. To explain this point, they wrote:

> Righteousness can here only be something people have, namely, their obedient, righteous conduct; 'justification' and 'vindication' are both excluded. So in 5.10 'righteousness' has demonstrably to do with God's demand, not God's gift. This is important for interpreting the other occurrences of δικαιοσυνη in Matthew which are more ambiguous (see further Przybyiski, pp. 98-9).[207]

The above statement sets the stage for their final position on verse 10, where they too conclude with Albright and Mann that this passage is *inclusio*. Thereby, "the *inclusio* also implies that the promises in beatitudes 2-7 are all different ways of saying the same thing, namely, 'theirs is the kingdom of heaven,' the promise of the first and eighth beatitudes."[208] Davies and Allison thus take a structural view of the passages, because they seem to have felt very strongly that verse 10 is simply a transitional bridge to verses 11 and 12. However, they do not finish their own argument: that the "transition" can be understood as a reference to the specifically rabbinic practices of teaching.

In his commentary, Randolph Yeager believes that it is important to make one final point comparing a Hellenistic interpretation of that passage (based on a particular understanding of moral virtues, and of textual exegesis) with one based on the Semitic position that stresses real historical references. In fact, Yeager writes a very long comment on this passage, one that is important to view for the understanding of how this culture influences scholarship even to this day. Yeager writes:

> Jesus is talking about the immediate future when righteousness is going to be met with social disapproval. We detect the shadow of the cross in this and the two verses which follow. Here is another example of Jesus' philosophy cutting across the current teaching of the Scribes and Pharisees with respect to the kingdom. They were expecting the imminent establishment of Messiah's Kingdom of Heavens, which was to be characterized by universal righteousness *Cf*. Isa. 11:9, Jer. 31:34 and many other kingdom prophecies which agree in describing the kingdom as one wherein men would be righteous and wherein virtue would be extolled and rewarded. But here Jesus begins to talk to men about being persecuted for righteousness' sake. The society that persecutes the righteous cannot be said to be a righteous society. Jesus, of course, knew the future program of the Godhead, and the state

of the unregenerate hearts of Israel's leaders. He is therefore prophesying that the righteous are in for persecution at the hands of the unrighteous and says that they should be happy that this is so, and should regard it as an honor, because the kingdom of the heavens will belong to the persecuted and not to the persecutors. He intensifies the thought in verse 11. To righteousness brings persecution. Both the righteousness (vs. 6) and the persecution which it brings (vss. 11,12) bring happiness, however. Hence it is a double blessedness. The seven characters here described are all in the teeth of the spirit of the world, insomuch that such hearers of this discourse as breathed that spirit must have been startled, and had their whole system of thought and action rudely dashed. Poverty of spirit runs counter to the pride of men's heart; a pensive disposition, in the view of one's universal deficiencies before God is ill relished by the callous, indifferent, laughing, self-satisfied world; a meek and quiet spirit, taking wrong, is regarded as pusillanimous and rasps against the proud, resentful spirit of the world; that craving after spiritual blessings rebukes but too unpleasantly the lust of the flesh, the lust of the eye and the pride of life; so does a merciful spirit the hardheartedness of the world; purity of heart contrasts painfully with painted hypocrisy, and the peacemaker cannot easily be endured by the contentious, quarrelsome world. Thus does 'righteousness' come to be 'persecuted.' But blessed are they who, in spite of this, dare to be righteous. Jesus is suggesting that to follow Him is to take up a cross (Mt. 16:24), endure its offence (Gal. 5:11) and share with Him the hatred of the unregenerate world (John 15:18; I John 3:13; I Pet. 4:12,13). The most severe indictment that could be brought against society is the fact that when there came a man like Jesus to live on this planet, who taught the kind of philosophy found in these opening verses, they murdered Him.[209]

The above quotes are important because it ties the issues discussed in the previous chapter to those being discussed here, and establishes how each are dependent upon the Hellenized approach. New Testament scholars almost exclusively turn to the assumption that the text is either theological or philosophical. They, rather than reflecting upon the historical setting and the circumstances of that culture, focus on the traditional teachings produced during the German school of thought (the Enlightenment period). The uses of Hellenistic positions has brought about a painful effort to distinguish itself from its true Jewish Christian beginning. Instead, there is yet another indictment that future historians will bring to the forefront in discussing such critical scholarship, that of the failure of modern New Testament scholars to perpetuate or to even acknowledge the historical roots of the Jewish/Christian beliefs. While such contributions by the German scholars produced hermeneutical principles to analyze biblical text, it is difficult to understand why such principles were not applied to a Jewish history that gave birth to the God of our Lord and Savior Jesus. Again, instead, these tools such as Form, Source, Redaction, Canon, and Textual Criticisms, were the exegetical methodologies used to embrace the Greco-Rome culture in which the Biblical text emerged. While scholars such as Lindsey and Flusser, using the same criticisms, have unlocked first century biblical interpretations that are now allowing others to study the Gospels and to hear Jesus speak as though they were sitting at the feet of the Master today.

Thus that historicizing approach is imperative for understanding these last two Beatitudes. In juxtaposing the positions of Donald Hagner, W. F. Albright and C. S. Mann, W. D. Davies and Dale C. Allison, and Randolph O. Yeager, with that of the Hebraic school of thought, something very beautiful emerges in the interpretation of Matthew 5:10. First the word persecute, in which the above scholars struggled in considering its uses in Matthew 5:10, is not the same word being used in the Hebrew text. Again, the solution to this dilemma is found in scholarship that acknowledges parallels between the Bible passages and newer sources like that of the Dead Sea Scrolls. For example, in the book by Bivin and Blizzard they correctly point out that Christian scholars are mistakenly interpreting the word persecution as meaning a type of theological martyrdom. Such is the case of our New Testament commentators, already sited. Millions had gone to their death believing that suffering was a religious merit, and that they were being persecuted for the sake of God's kingdom.

However, according to Bivin and Blizzard, there are four mistranslations in Matthew 5:10. The first mistake is that, in this beatitude, Jesus is not discussing the concept *persecute* as it occurred in verses 11 and 12. The Hebrew word used in this verse הגרדפים from the root word רדף is instead defined as *pursue, chase, persecute.*[210] Parallel examples of the above definition can be seen in the following passages:

> Psalms 38:20-21: Those who repay my good with evil slander me when I **pursue** what is good. O Lord, do not forsake me: be not far from me, O my God (NIV).

> I Samuel 23:28: Wherefore Saul returned from **pursuing** after David, and went against the Philistines: therefore they called that place Sela-hammahlekoth (NKJ).

Psalms 71:11: They say, 'God has forsaken him; **persue** him and seize him, for no one will rescue him' (NIV).

Psalms 71:11: Saying, God hath forsaken him: **persecute** (follow) and take him; for there is none to deliver him (NKJ).

Psalms 35:6: May their path be dark and slippery, with the angel of the Lord **pursuing** them (NIV).

Psalms 35:6: Let their way be dark and slippery: and let the angel of the Lord **persecute** them (NKJ).

Psalms 23:6: Surely goodness and mercy shall **follow** me all the days of my life: and I will dwell in the house of the Lord for ever (NKJ).

Psalms 119:150: They draw nigh that **follow** after mischief: they are far from thy law (NKJ).

Isaiah 51:1: Listen to me, you who **pursue** righteousness and who seek the Lord: Look to the rock from which you were cut and to the quarry from which you were hewn (NIV).

Isaiah 51:1: Hearken to me, ye that **follow** after righteousness, ye that seek the Lord: look unto the rock whence ye are hewn, and to the hole of the pit whence ye are digged (NKJ).

The above passages are excellent illustrations of how רדף was often used in a manner in which *persecute* contextually makes no sense as being translated by Hellenistic scholars.

Such is the case in Matthew 5:10, where Hagner, Davies and Allison, Yeager, and Albright and Mann all espouse positions which resemble that of the eclectic Greek text to which their interpretations are formed. Isaiah 51:1 is the most probable text to which Jesus was hinting (*remez*) in verse 10. The text reads: *Listen to me, you who pursue righteousness*, which parallels Jesus' words in verse 10, *Happy are those who pursue righteousness*, as in the case of those who run after God's *vindication*, God's *redemption*, God's *salvation*, and God's *justification*. Accordingly, these are the individuals who make up the Kingdom of Heaven or God's Kingdom. Bivin and Blizzard point to the other three mistranslations that have blocked this reading, by saying:

> Secondly, "righteousness" is an unfortunate translation in English. "Salvation" or "redemption" would be more accurate, Thirdly, "theirs" also leaves the wrong impression. We do not possess the Kingdom. The correct translation would be "of these," or "of such as these" as in Luke 18:16, "Let the children come to me and do not prevent them, for *of such as these* is the Kingdom of God." Fourthly, the Kingdom of Heaven is not futuristic, as is so often understood. In the eighth beatitude Jesus is not discussing persecution at all. He is describing people whose chief desire is for God to redeem the world. The Beatitudes are a description of the kind of people who make up the kingdom of Heaven. This beatitude, like the others, characterizes the "Kingdom Man," who wants above all else for God to rule in the life of every person. The eighth beatitude echoes the fourth beatitude which speaks of those who "hunger and thirst [i.e., 'desire above all else'] for righteousness," in other words, for God to save the

lost. It also echoes Matthew 6:33 in which Jesus says that we are to "seek first [i.e., 'desire above all else'] His righteousness [i.e., 'salvation']."[211]

In the statement above, Bivin and Blizzard assume a Semitic point of view for interpreting this passage, one which allowed them to capture the meaning of Matthew 5:10 more as the audience of Jesus' day would have heard it. In the traditions of the Rabbis, Jesus employed the great rabbinic style of teaching, familiar to those hearing his message. Unfortunately, before and after the canonization of the New Testament, that message became polluted. Instead of New Testament scholars utilizing all available historical sources, as we have seen, a Hellenized culture replaced the roots of the newly birthed Christian movement, and thus scholars have overlooked this clear reference to a movement of a kingdom of this earth, to that of the future or hereafter.

The Hebrew Scriptures in the book of Psalms provide additional evidence supporting a Hebraic text under the Greek text. In Psalms 23:3 the expression, *he guides me in paths of righteousness for his name's sake*, a Hebraism closely parallels that of Matthew 5:10. The text reads "He guides me in the path of righteousness"; thus this Hebraism can be understood more clearly in the following readings: He guides me in the paths of His vindication, of His salvation, of His redemption, of His deliverance for His name's sake. Hence, it is possible to say: *Happy are those who are being guided to display righteousness in their actions, for his name's sake, they make up His kingdom; or happy are those who are guided in the paths (running after doing acts of) vindication, redemption, salvation, for his name's sake.* This rewriting speaks to a possible expansion of the passage that stresses behaviors that redeem the value of a good life on this earth, not just because of the Lord's wrath

– a much more life-affirming reading, stressing the following of a good path rather than fear of retribution.

A contemporary Hebraic translation of Matthew 5:10 might thus read: *Happy are those who are running after God's salvation, redemption, deliverance, for these are the people over whom God is ruling now, for these are they that make up the Kingdom of Heaven.*

Matthew 5:11

> Matthew 5:11: *Blessed are ye, when men shall revile you, and persecute you, and shall say all manner of evil against you falsely, for my sake.*

In the commentary, John Trapp picks up on the meaning of persecute as defined in verse 10, to pursue or follow, and applies this meaning to verse 11, as well. However, unlike verse 10, where the term persecution is associated with righteousness. Trapp associates the use of persecute in this verse with the image of a hunter, hunting his prey.

This diametrically opposed reading points to an underlying problem in the scholarship on Matthew 5:11. The most crucial issue is its provenance. Douglas Hare suggested that, because this beatitude differs in form from the other eight, thus it can be credited to "editorial activity on the part of the Evangelists or previous transmitters of the tradition."[212] Hare also states:

> If this hypothetical reconstruction is correct, Matthew has introduced two interesting changes. First, the verb "persecute," already employed in verse 10, is introduced at two different points (it is absent from Luke's version). Second, the phrase "the ones before you" is appended to "the prophets." Matthew's intention can be glimpsed

by comparing his revised beatitude with 23:34: "Therefore I send you prophets and wise men and scribes, some whom you will...persecute from town to town" (see also 10:23). The Evangelist apparently regarded Christian missionaries who proclaimed the gospel to fellow Jews as standing within the prophetic traditions. A frequently hostile response was to be expected, in view of the tradition that Israel always persecutes its prophets (see II Chro. 36:15-16; Neh. 9:26; Acts 7:52).[213]

In this statement, Hare interpreted Matthew's version of the beatitude as resting on an "unhappy experience of Jewish-Christian missionaries."[214] One must ask the question: was there any such person (as a Jewish-Christian missionary) during the time Matthew's text was being written? This is clearly an assumption on the part of Hare whose rendering, not surprisingly of verse 10, rests on Hellenistic teachings that Paul was sent out as a missionary. For the most extensive explanation of why this statement is totally incorrect, see Brad H. Young, *Paul, The Jewish Theologian: A Pharisee among Christians, Jews and Gentiles*, Young writes concerning Paul:

The New Testament describes the Apostle Paul as a Pharisee who comes to faith in Jesus as the Messiah, boldly proclaiming the gospel as the power of the God of Israel unto salvation, to the diverse peoples in distant parts of a Gentile world. Working in a largely pagan environment, the one who is referred to in the book of Acts as Saul of Tarsus establishes churches as the Apostle Paul. Paul has been referred to as the "second founder of Christianity." He has been called a "mystic." Now he is referred to as "Gnostic." The consensus of scholarship has come to view him as a Hellenistic Jew who departed radically from his Judaism. Scholars view him as being influenced by his upbringing in the Stoic environs of Tarsus and various streams of thought flowing forth from paganism, Greco-Roman culture, popular Hellenistic philosophy, mystery religious cults, and Gnostic systems. Seldom is the origin of Paul's faith seen as rooted in Pharisaism.[215]

Within the statement above it is important to ask (according to Hare) which group of Pharisees are involved. For the politics of the relationship of the Jewish Christians and the Hellenistic Christians is more complicated than a simple dichotomy of accepting or refuting traditional Judaic precepts.

In one sense, Paul does indeed fulfill Hare's reading of verse 11, by being a persecutor of those spoken of in this verse. Thus it seems to be necessary for Hare's own consistency, since, just as he and other Hellenistic New Testament scholars believed, Paul was the first missionary to the Gentiles, a promulgated theology used for supporting their claim. To this end, Young records the words of Abraham Joshua Heschel, who addresses this mythology of all Christians rejecting all Jews with these words:

> The Christian message, which in its origins intended to be an affirmation and culmination of Judaism, became very early diverted into a repudiation and negation of Judaism; obsolescence and abrogation of Jewish faith became conviction and doctrine; the new covenant was conceived not as a new phase or disclosure but as abolition and replacement of the ancient one; theological thinking fashioned its

terms in a spirit of antithesis to Judaism. Contrast and contradiction rather than acknowledgement of roots relatedness and indebtedness, became the perspective. Judaism a religion of law, Christianity a religion of grace; Judaism teaches a God of wrath, Christianity a God of love; Judaism a religion of slavish obedience, Christianity the conviction of free men; Judaism is particularism, Christianity is universalism; Judaism seeks works-righteousness, Christianity preaches faith-righteousness. The teaching of the old covenant a religion of fear, the gospel of the new covenant a religion of love.[216]

Instead of placing Paul in his historical setting, therefore, he is taken as being called by God to join those who were persecuted as the followers of Christ. Thus in Hellenistic scholarship, Paul is seen cast in a role of Greco-Roman perspective wherein he rejected his Jewish background.

The result for this scholarship is familiar. A whole theology is built on the mentality of suffering for the sake of a future hope (kingdom) – for a kingdom defined in the Hellenistic view rather than in a Jewish-Christian tradition. John Lange exemplifies this mentality, as he argues:

By pointing to the great reward in heaven, the Lord sets the fact more clearly than ever before His hearers, that the kingdom of Messiah is not of this world, and that perfectness will only be attained there, while here we are to prepare for it by suffering and witness-bearing on behalf of Christ.[217]

Thus the reward of heaven is given to them that encounter suffering on the account or for the sake of Christ. Making a similar point, Randolph Yeager said, "Christians are to consider themselves fortunate at whatever future time they are persecuted, maligned and slandered as a result of their identification with Christ and His kingdom."[218]

This theological interpretation can easily stand for many subsequent ones that support the Hellenized Christians' principle of suffering for Christ. Yeager's comments on this passage provide the Christian perspective with what he interprets to be the proper reaction. Stressing persecution as a kind of battle, he writes:

> When the enemy says the unkind things to us, they will be lying when they say it. Peter warns that Christians may be criticized justly (I Pet. 4:15). Jesus is talking about the suffering that comes to us as Christians (I Pet. 4:16). God's children are not promised blessing if the world truthfully criticizes us and then deals out punishment on a just basis. The victorious Christian will give no occasion for just criticism. But when the unregenerate world says "every evil thing against us" and are lying when they say it, then we are happy (blessed). *Cf.* verse 10 for the previous use of ἐνεκὲν "Because of righteousness" and "Because of me." Thus Christ is identified with righteousness (I Cor. 1:30). Verse 11 is an intensification and restatement of verse 10.
>
> There Jesus inferred that the time was coming when righteousness would be persecuted and He, as incarnate righteousness, would be crucified by the very men of the establishment who professed righteousness to the highest degree! Later Jesus was to say that the righteousness of His kingdom exceeded that of the establishment. (Mat. 5:20). Jesus now associates Himself with the righteousness of God and thus makes His claim to be a fulfillment

of the law (Mt. 5:17). He prophesied that He will be rejected and that His followers also will be rejected and further that this rejection will be caused by His righteous standard and that of His followers.[219]

Thus the logic of the above statement is therefore straightforward. Happy is the reward, and happy is the reaction Christians use to carry themselves through times of suffering. Yeager goes on to associate verses 17 and 20 with Matthew 5:11, in that it is a fulfillment of the reward of righteousness given to those who are persecuted.

Note that these readings all hinge on the assumption that "persecution" is meant to be understood in relation to hunter and hunted, as opposed to its other meaning, "to follow after." While the position held by Robert Lindsey juxtaposed to that of Randolph Yeager on verse 11 provides a clear contrast which emerges in the interpretation of this passage. Lindsey's position is rooted in the differences between Jewish and Hellenistic thought that have been traced already in early chapters. Lindsey writes:

From Matthew 5:11, 12 and Luke 6:22, 23 we see that the Reorganized Scroll tended often to put sayings together on the basis of some word or idea. Where the word "persecuted" appeared in the eighth beatitude in Matthew (5:10) the author of this scroll combined a further saying about persecution, but this time, in contrast to the beatitude, you (plural) is used:

"Blessed are you when men revile you and persecute you and cast your name out as evil (a Hebraism preserved by Luke but not by Matthew and meaning to give a bad name to someone) because of the Son of Man."

Normally none would enjoy being made fun of and laughed at, but Jesus calls his people to treat those that despise them as sources of joy for this is because they are associated with him. They are laughing at you. Turn it all around, and laugh yourself.

"Rejoice and be glad, for your reward is great in heaven, for in the same way men used to persecute the prophets who were before you" (Matthew 5:12; Luke 6:23).

Nor is Jesus just glorifying suffering. Look at his words of warning about how to know if you are dealing at any given time with someone likely to cause you harm. He is probably talking about the circumstances under which they are to give their testimony.[220]

According to Lindsey, Jesus is telling his followers there will come a time when they will face conditions of hostility, because they follow him. In verse 11, the Hebrew word יחרפו from the root word חרף is defined as *reproach,* as in "to say sharply against." Thus a more literal rendering of verse 11 can be *happy are you when men speak harshly, violently at you.*

In this passage יחרפו and ירדפו can be interpreted as being a combination of a single action, an interaction that represents both reviling and persecution – an action and response of two individuals or two parties, not just a unilateral action from a hostile outside. The textual evidence supports this more transactional reading. In verse 11, the Hebrew word וידברו *and they say,* as in speaking, is key to understanding the reflective actions of both reviled and persecuted. In the above statement Lindsey translates part of verse 11, *and cast your name out as evil*, as another Hebraism. In Luke 6:22, *and cast out your name as evil* is a Hebrew idiom, one which, according to Bivin and Blizzard, should be understood as implying a distinct social transaction, not just a moral judgment. Their justification is extensive, but it is a fine example of how Hebrew underpinnings of the Bible (not Greek) verses become very significant. They argue:

> The idiom has not been preserved perfectly, since the word "as" is not part of the idiom. In Hebrew it is not "name as evil" (or "bad"), but simply "name bad" (*shem rah*). Why? Because in Hebrew adjectives follow nouns. In English one says "narrow street." In Hebrew one says "street narrow." In English one says "bad name" – in Hebrew, "name bad." The Greek translator of the Hebrew biography was a firm believer in literal translations, but to write in Greek "Cast out your name *as* bad," he hoped to make his translation more intelligible to his Greek readers. There is a further difficulty. Even if we remove the word "as," and correctly translate "bad name" instead of "name bad," this expression is still not clear in English. What does "Cast out your bad name" mean? "Cast out" is a very poor English translation, not because it is not a legitimate translation of the Greek verb used here, but because it is not a translation, as it should be, of the Hebrew equivalent of that Greek verb. As was customary, the Greek translator employed the fixed or standard Greek translation of a Hebrew word rather than trying to translate to idiomatic Greek. Unfortunately the Greek verb used here (*ekballo*), and its Hebrew equivalent (*hotzi*) is a causative form of a root meaning "go out." This form of the Hebrew verb may therefore be translated literally

as "come to go (or come) out," but may also often mean "cause to go out" in the sense of "make public" or "publish." It is obvious that the latter meaning is demanded in this context.

"Publish (or publicize) your name bad" is simply a Hebrew way of saying "defame you," "malign you," or "slander you." The phrase traditionally translated in English by six words, "cast out your name as evil," is a Hebrew idiom which, if English translators would only seek Hebrew equivalents to the Greek, could be translated in English by only two words: "malign you." And should an English translator wish to find equivalent English idioms that preserve some of the literalness of the Hebrew expression, such as the word "name," he has at his disposal, in colloquial English, expressions such as "give you a bad name," or "smear your name." "When you are slandered on my account," Jesus says, "rejoice, for great is your reward in heaven."[221]

In this statement, the final part of the interpretation of Matthew v. 11, might be interpreted: *happy are you even when men violently, harshly speak of you, and they publicly defame you, slander you for my sake. They are not speaking this way because of you, but because of me; therefore you should rejoice.* That is, the passage is directed towards an individual affirming, following, a belief that is part of the old and new community, rather than a renunciation of an older identity. Here again, the more familiar reading of the passage stresses a continuation of an historical condition redefined to meet the needs of those becoming a part of newer phases of the believing communities of the first millennium.

There is yet another possible interpretation of this verse; it also focuses on the Hebrew behind the Greek text. The Greek word for 'reproach' is ονειδισωσιν from the root ονειδος and according to Edwin Hatch and Henry A. Redpath, *A Concordance to the Septuagint*, there are five Hebrew words that translate this one Greek word. One of the five comes from the root word חרף which is found in the Hebrew translation of verse 11, and also used in Hosea 12:14, *Ephraim provoked him to anger most bitterly: therefore shall he leave his blood upon him, and his reproach shall his Lord return unto him.* Similarly, the other Greek word in verse 11, (διωξωσιν from the root διωκω or διωκειν in the LXX), according to Hatch and Redpath, is translated by thirteen different Hebrew words. One of these is the root רדף; see Jeremiah 15:15, *You understand, O Lord; remember me and care for me. Avenge me of my persecutors, You are long suffering, do not take me away; think of how I suffer reproach for your sake.* In this passage we are discussing both מרדפי and חרפה are used, and they parallel to the usages in Matthew 5:11. That multiplicity of meanings in the context of the redefinition of "persecution" as "following" offers a second reading of this passage, one which might read: *happy are you when men pursue you to slander you, and cast down your name as evil in public, for my sake.*

A contemporary Hebraic translation might make this reading of Matthew 5:11; *Happy are you when they slander and they persecute you, and they speak in deception of You, for my sake.*

This reading would, again, represent a translation of the underlying Hebrew concepts into a more appropriate form, one capturing its reference to a specific political and social climate. This Beatitude speaks of a kind of individual honor that accrues to those who stand up for their beliefs, not an acceptance of being hunted as prey.

Final Analysis of Persecution

The persecution addressed by the last two Beatitudes would, in my reading, have offered rabbis teaching on the topics considerably more latitude to discuss community identity and social justice than Hellenized scholars would assume today. Unfortunately, these passages do not carry the same weight as in a Hebraic context. They are speaking considerably more simply, referring to relations within a community. They recommend that individuals follow a right path, pursuing their beliefs, and that it is a noble thing to do in the face of resistance. What was interpersonal advice, therefore, has been transformed into a much more inflated political statement, one that obscures what is a normal piece of rabbinic advice behind the assumed complete break of Jesus' followers from their Judaic roots.

NOTES FOR CHAPTER 7

[203]Hagner, p. 96: "These declarations of happiness are to some extent a manifestation of realized eschatology. The remarkable tension throughout is, of course, caused by the temporary delay of the final consummation. In this interim period those who may appear to enjoy anything but the favor of God are paradoxically blessed. In their present condition, and even as they experience intense persecution, they are already accounted as supremely happy. Salvation has begun; their time has come, and this assurance of the future is meant to transform their present existence."

[204]Lagne, p. 103: "In ver. 3, we have the kingdom of heaven with all that is implied, – here, with all that it imparts; there, as objectively set before us, – here, as our own personal and actual possession."

[205]Albright and Mann, p. 13.

[206]Davies and Allison, p. 459.

[207]Davies and Allison, p. 460.

[208]Davies and Allison, p. 460: "Yet if 5.10, through the device of repetition, is bound to what precedes it, the verse also points forward by virtue of its subject matter, persecution, to 5. 11-12, for persecution is also the subject matter of these two verses."

[209]Yeager, pp. 341-342.

[210]Brown-Driver-Briggs, p. 922: "1a pursue in order to overtake...2 follow after, aim to secure."

[211]Bivin and Blizzard, p. 76: "In Matthew 5:10 Jesus is again emphasizing that the kind of people who make up the Kingdom of God are those who want more than anything else to see God save the lost, those who pray 'Thy Kingdom come' (an exhortation which means 'Rule God, over more and more individuals).'"

[212]Hare, p. 43: "When such alterations are subtracted, the earlier version emerges as follows: 'Blessed are you when they revile you and slander you because of me. Rejoice and exult, because your reward is great in heaven, for so they did to the prophets.'"

[213]Hare, p. 43.

[214]Hare, p. 43: "Christians who take their faith seriously and consequently are impelled to take a stand on moral issues and to support controversial or unpopular cause must expect to be ridiculed and maligned. Such hostility is unpleasant but not crushing to those who are convinced that God's approbation is more important by far than fleeting popularity. The solitary crusader finds solace in the dictum, 'One with God constitutes a majority.'"

[215]Young, *Paul the Jewish Theologian*, p. 1: "This book begins with a different set of presuppositions. Paul calls himself a Pharisee. We should listen to what Paul tells us about himself. In fact, there is no evidence anywhere in the New Testament that he departed from his firm convictions as a Pharisee. Paul is a Jewish theologian

who anchored his beliefs in the Hebrew Bible and the teachings of his eminent mentors in Jerusalem. He is a Hebrew of the Hebrews rather than a Hellenist of the Greeks. Fresh evidence from the literary discoveries of the Dead Sea Scrolls as well as renewed interest in the analysis of rabbinic literature place the Apostle Paul squarely within the land of Israel and not the Hellenism of Asia Minor, although surely there was much interaction between Hellenism and Judaism in the first century and this influenced Pharisaism. Paul is a Pharisee who has been rejected by the synagogue and misunderstood by the church."

[216]Young, p.3.

[217]Lange, p. 103: "Blessed are ye when men shall revile you, etc. for my sake. – This is the special application of what the Lord had above declared, or the interpretation of the language used in ver. 10."

[218]Yeager, p. 345.

[219]Yeager, p. 345.

[220]Lindsey, p. 184: "You have joined the great prophets. They had lots of troubles and so will you! You just have to laugh when Jesus says it! But many have proved it works! Smile and the world smiles with you, weep and you weep alone! Victory lies in the lap of the persecuted, not the persecutor."

[221]Bivin and Blizzard, pp. 116-117.

[222]Lindsey, pp. 61-62: "Imagine my surprise when one day as I came to see Flusser for a couple of hours of study he looked up to me from his desk, cluttered with books, and said, 'Lindsey, I think I know what biazetai means! In fact, I know what it means!' 'Fine, what is it?' I could only ask. 'Look,' he said seriously, 'I was looking up something Radak mentioned.' Radak is the name by which a famous medieval rabbi and commentator is known. 'I am all ears,' I said. 'Biazetai is a translation

of poretz!' he almost shouted, waving a Hebrew Bible at me. Radak mentions an old interpretation on Micah 2:13. Look at Micah 2:12 and 13. I read it. I will surely gather all of you, O Jacob... like sheep in a fold, like a flock in its pasture, a noisy multitude of men. The breaker (poretz) will go up before them; they will break through and pass the gate, going out by it. Their king will pass on before them, The Lord at their head."

[223]Joseph Frankovic, *The Kingdom of Heaven* (Tulsa, OK: HaKesher, Inc. 1998), p. 6.

[224]Pocock, p. 22: "Pococke was born on November 8, 1604 to a Berkshire clergyman. He received his secondary education from Oxford, where he began to focus on Oriental studies under M. Pasor and W. Bedwell. In 1630 Pocock sailed for Aleppo in order to serve as chaplain of the English factory there. During this time, he acquired great skill in the Arabic tongue and improved his knowledge of Syriac and Ethiopic. Knowledge of these languages and Hebrew, which he studied at Oxford, made rabbinic literature accessible to him. He was particularly impressed with the literature written in Arabic...In 1676 and 1677 his commentaries on Micah and Malachi were published. These were followed by commentaries on Hosea in 1685 and Joel in 1691, In these works Pocock quotes extensively from the Rabbis of his day and the writings of their predecessors. He loved and knew thoroughly the Hebrew scriptures and the literature of the Jewish people. In the preface of his Micah commentary, Pocock writes, "[The Oriental studies] which of late, if not all along, hath had that unhappiness, as to be scarce able to keep itself, not only from neglect, but contempt, as needless; at least of no great use or necessity." This great man, who labored in study and pastoral duties throughout his life while being harassed by enemies and abandoned

by friends but respected for purity of life and matchless learning, died on September 10, 1691 at the age of 87. J. H. Worman, *Encyclopaedia Britanica*, vol. 24 (New York: Charles Scribner's Sons, 1885), pp. 252-255. Frankovic, p. 17.

[225]Flusser, *Jesus*, p. 266: "A movement had begun in Israel, the realization of the kingdom of heaven on earth (Matt. 6:10). The movement necessarily centered around the person of Jesus; separate initiatives, independent of Jesus, would not gather but scatter. One can recognize again how important the concepts of the kingdom of God among mankind – with the aid of colaborers."

[226]Lindsey, *Jesus Rabbi & Lord*, p. 62: "'Radak retains this old Midrash on the Messiah,' said Flusser. 'He says that 'the Breaker' is Elijah who precedes the coming of the Messiah, the 'king' is melech hemistich and 'the Lord' is of course the God of Israel.' Typical rabbinic exposition of a messianic passage. 'All the people of course know this text of Micah 2:13 refers to the Messiah,' continued Flusser. 'Jesus hints at it as he so often does in other passages.' (pp. 62-63).

[227]Flusser, *Jesus*, p. 91: "The same is true with the Sermon on the Mount in which Jesus presumably defines his own personal attitude towards the law of Moses (Matt. 5:17-48). In the sermon, Jesus in a certain sense brings things old and new out of his granary. The sensitivity within ancient Judaism evolved a whole dialectic of sin, in contrast to the simple view of the Old Testament. When man ceases to be regarded as an unproblematic being, sins themselves become a problem. If a person is not careful, one sin can lead to another. Even an action that does not appear sinful can cause him to become entangled in a real sin. There was a saying, 'Flee from what is evil and from what resembles evil.' If we apply this concept to the commandments, we

discover that the lesser commandments are as serious as the greater. Jesus' exegesis in Matt. 5:17-48 should be understood in this sense. The exegesis proper is preceded by a preamble (Matt. 5:17-20) where Jesus justifies his method."

[228]Young, Paul, *The Jewish Theologian*, p. 63.

[229]Young, p. 63: "In contrast to Marcion, Jesus and Paul valued Torah. Here we will examine the words of Jesus in Matt. 5:17 and of Paul in Rom 3:31. The deep roots of these two key verses in Judaism are sometimes overlooked. When this happens our opinions of the law run the risk of becoming tainted by vestiges of Marcion's towering influence."

[230]Bivin and Blizzard, pp. 112-113: "And what was it that was lacking in the Law? The Messiah. Jesus fulfilled the Law, that is, he fulfilled the messianic prophecies found in the Law (and the prophets). In other words, in Jesus, the Law reached its zenith. Rather than being destroyed, it now existed as God originally intended. It had come to an end in one form, but continued in another, more perfect form."

[231]Bivin and Blizzard, p. 92: "Another Hebraism to which the English speaker would be insensitive, but which would definitely jar a Greek speaker: a verb of motion followed by an infinitive – in this case the verb 'come' followed by the infinitive 'to cast.' This is perfectly good Hebrew syntax, yet altogether foreign to Greek. To our surprise, though the Gospels of Matthew, Mark, and Luke were written in Greek, we find scattered throughout these Gospels numerous examples of the construction verb of motion plus infinitive. 'He stood up to read' in Luke 4:16 is another example (verb of motion, 'stood up,' plus infinitive, 'to read'). A small point, perhaps, and one easily overlooked, but another strong indication that behind our Greek text is a Hebrew original."

[232]Bivin and Blizzard, p. 113.

[233]Bivin and Blizzard, p. 114.

[234]Bivin and Blizzard, p. 110.

[235]Bivin and Blizzard, p. 111: "And what is the Kingdom of Heaven? We must remember that the Kingdom of Heaven is not futuristic. 'Kingdom of Heaven' is Jesus' name for his movement, the body of his disciples; and 'to enter or come into the Kingdom of Heaven' means to become a disciple or believer, (It does not mean "to go to heaven.") If your righteousness is reduced to almsgiving, Jesus admonished, you will not be in my movement, the Kingdom of Heaven. If it is your tsedakah, and not God's tsedakah, you will miss God's tsedakah (salvation) altogether. You will not find it because you will be looking for it in the wrong place."

[236]Eli Yassif, *The Sacrifice of Isaac: Studies in the Development of a Literary Tradition* (Jerusalem: Makor Publishing, Ltd., n.d.) p. 17.

[237]C.F. Evans, *The Cambridge History of the Bible vol. I* (Cambridge: Univ. Press, 1970) p. 229.

CONCLUSION

The examples discussed in the above chapters range from a discussion of The Kingdom of Heaven as it reveals the political and cultural setting of early Jewish Christianity, to the alternate translations of the Beatitudes. I have suggested that their underlying social and theological senses should not be falsified as part of the image of a Christian church that did not yet exist in that form. My examples, I believe, point to a compelling problem for the present generation and scholars.

Currently scholars of the Hebraic Studies are publishing texts and setting forth new directions for Biblical research, particularly in response to revelations by the Dead Sea Scrolls. Accordingly, students from every walk of life and from every region of the world are beginning to heed the Hebraic call for academic Biblical research based on Semitic sources. In many, if not most cases, they are driven by an unquenchable thirst to return to the original roots of their Christian birth. These students are taking their positions, like scholars of yesterday, in this exciting field of study. They too are positioning themselves for academic contributions that will help shape beliefs for generations to come.

Yet, as shown in reference to many existing commentaries, many of these scholars have not managed to reclaim these Semitic roots as relating to real historical situations or to theological and social debates configured within those situations. In the ongoing field of Hebraic research let it be stated that this new generation of scholars must uphold different claims, which has already become evident today. Among these are not only a full account of Hebrew sources in relation to the Greek and Latin ones that are most familiar, but also an acknowledgment that each translation and interpretation is itself subject to a kind of drift, be that drift conscious or unconscious. As Lefevere notes in the work on cultural translation cited in the first section, each translation or "reading" is an appropriation of the original text that answers not only to the source material, but also to the needs of the audience for which it is intended.

In this context, a great debt of thanks is due those who began the latest infusion of Hebraic influence in Biblical studies, especially in scholarship on the Gospels of Matthew, Mark, Luke, and the first 15 chapters of Acts. Perhaps most notable among these is Dr. Robert Lisle Lindsey (deceased) who left his family, friends, and colleagues 31 May 1995. In searching for a clear interpretation of the text, Lindsey began to work with a methodology which has unlocked the Hebraic meanings that are behind the Greek text. Dr. Lindsey's contribution is immeasurable, and yet he is only one among a growing number of scholars who recognized the importance of viewing these texts in the original Hebrew language. Another scholar whose contributions pre-date Lindsey but who already saw the value in translating the text from its native historical roots was Edward Pococke in *A Commentary on the Prophesy of Micah* (1676). His knowledge of Biblical Hebrew opened many doors to students desiring to research the text from a Hebraic format.

An example of how these works by Lindsey and Pococke complement each other, despite their distance in time, can be seen in a reconstructed pericope on Matthew 11:12, *And from the days of John the Baptist until now the kingdom of heaven suffered violence, and the violent take it by force.* Lindsey records that, during his early stages of learning, he noted that there was a Hebrew text beneath the Greek Gospels. He met with a colleague, David Flusser, who confirmed that, beneath the Greek word βιασται, there was a Hebrew word with a completely differently meaning. Lindsey recalls:

> Almost anyone who reads these words wonders what they mean, commentators included. I remember many years ago trying for hours at a time guessing about one solution or another. A well-known volume entitled The Jerusalem Bible has these notes at the bottom of the page where this passage occurs:
>
> Various interpretations have been offered. The violence may be:
> 1. ...the bitter self-sacrifice of those who would take possession of the kingdom;
> 2. ...the misguided violence of those who would establish the kingdom by force (the Zealots);
> 3. ...the tyrannical violence of the powers of evil...
>
> It is clear that none of these solutions makes much sense. I remember thinking once that perhaps what Jesus meant was that only the very aggressive could manage to get into the Kingdom of God. That was so unlike the man from Galilee, who

said, that I decided my solution was as bad as the others I had seen. One thing that intrigued me several years ago was the possibility that the Greek word, which is usually rendered "suffers violence" (*biazetai*) might not have a passive sense but an active sense. Perhaps, I guessed, it represents the Hebrew word *poretz*, but I concluded it was just a random thought of mine.[222]

In the above statement Lindsey credited Flusser for mentioning the text where *poretz* could be found. According to Lindsey and Flusser, *poretz* is found in Micah 2:13; the text reads: *The breaker is come up before them: they have broken up, and have passed through the gate, and are gone out by it: and their king shall pass before them, and the Lord on the head of them.* This connection opened up a whole arena of associations which Lindsey, Flusser, and others had to pursue.

For a more recent example, we can look to an article written by Joseph Frankovic, *The Kingdom of Heaven Breaks Forth, Matthew 11:12.* There he records a parallel passage from the Old Testament:

A titillating madras about Israel's redemption in the Messianic age is found in Pesikta Rabbati 35:4. The words "sing and rejoice" (Zech. 2:10-11) are taken as eschatological as pertaining to the time when the Holy one will redeem Israel. According to the madras, three days before Messiah comes, Elijah will stand upon the mountains of Israel and announce that Israel's redemption draws near. At the hour of redemption, the Holy One will show His glory and kingship to all the world. "He will redeem Israel, and He will appear at the head of them." Thus, it is said, "The breaker will go up before them…and the Lord will be at the head of them" (Micah 2:13). What makes this midrash particularly interesting is Radak's quotation of an earlier rabbinic source…This may be translated, "Our rabbis of blessed memory and the midrash teach, 'the breaker is Elijah and their king is the branch the Son of David.'" In addition to this, another midrash explaining Tamar's words, "Wherefore has thou made a breach for thyself" (Gen. 38:29), states that she meant: "This one (Perez) is greater than all who will make breaches, for from thee will arise [he of whom is written]," namely "the breaker" of Micah 2:13. It is apparent that a well established tradition of rabbinical interpretations focused upon the Messianic implications of Micah 2:13 and that the Hebrew mind attributed Messianic status to the title הפורץ. Thus, the question is asked. Did Jesus regard this title Messianically and implement it accordingly in His superlative teaching style?

In the statement above, Frankovic correctly points out that it is Jewish sources which clarify the meaning of those difficult words of the Gospels. In this case, the Midrash of Pesikta Rabbati addressed the redemptive purpose that would be a part of the Messianic age. Here we find a clear predisposition to identifying the historical Jesus with the concerns of the Hebrew nation of the era. An additional example of how important these connections are is in the way the passage confirms that, three days before the Messiah comes, the prophet Elijah will stand and proclaim that Israel's redemption draws near. Thus Matthew 11:12 is critical to our eventual understanding of these issues, because Edward Pococke confirmed that Jesus used the title *poretz* Messianically and that this "midrashim makes the phraseology of this verse 'more punctually applicable' than any other interpretation that may be postulated."[223] This verse is thus attributed to a teacher and a Messiah as defined in the era.

In Pococke's commentary on Micah he confirms in another way how the Bible itself clearly marks Jesus within his Hebraic context:

> But if any think, that by *Haporets*, "the breaker," and *Malcam*, "their King," should be meant two distinct persons, let him hear, what the Ancient Jew (as cited by the modern) say, for exposition of this place. *Haporets*, "the Breaker," that is Elisa, and *Malcam*, "their king," that is "the Branch," the Son of David; and then observe, what our Savior himself hath taught us, that John the Baptist was that Elias which was to come....
>
> And what our Savior saith, "This is he, of whom it is said, Behold, I send my Messenger before thy face, which shall prepare thy way before thee," and "that from the days of John the Baptist, the Kingdom of Heaven suffered violence, and the violent took it by force" Mat. 11.10, 12. Men breaking as it were, and passing through the gate, by his preaching repentance laid open, that they might go in and out: and it will be easy to apply to him this title of "the breaker." and so shall we have in the words, a most illustrious Prophecy of Christ, and his forerunner John the Baptist.[224]

In such passages, Pococke established that the breaker (also a metaphor for shepherd, see below) of Micah 2:13 is the same as Matthew 5:11-12. Thus again he opens up a new kind of crucial translation. Following his work, a new interpretation of Matthew 5:11-12 might read: *From the days of John the Baptist until now, the kingdom of heaven is breaking through and those who break through, take it in possession.*[225]

Quite naturally, then, the rest of the passage will flesh out the real circumstances of how this Son of Man related to his world. Lindsey gives an excellent example of this lengthy story in the Gospel of Matthew with these words:

> It was clear what the prophet was saying. God was comparing Israel to a flock kept up at night behind a temporary rock wall. In the morning the shepherd "breaks open" a gap in the wall and the sheep run pell-mell through the opening. But since he is really talking about people, the shepherd or "breaker" is both "their king before them" and "the Lord at their head."[226]

Thus here again, these important commentators make the kinds of connections between real circumstances and Bible verses that have been attributed only with speaking metaphorically.

The words of Jesus when viewed by using the Hebraic methodology will clearly help our understanding of the text. Look at two final passages that are difficult to interpret. They will further establish Hebrew as the key to proper understanding of the Gospel's message, not Greek. In Matthew 5:17 and 20 Jesus speaks:

> Think not that I am come to destroy the law, or the prophets; I am not come to destroy, but to fulfill.
>
> אל-תחשבו כי באתי להפר תא-התורה או תא-
> ברי הנביאים לם לא באתי להפר כי אם-מלאת
>
> For I say unto you, That except your righteousness shall exceed the righteousness of the scribes and

Pharisees, ye shall in no case enter into the kingdom of heaven.

כי אני אמר לכם אם לא־תרבה צדקתכם מצדקת
הסופרים והפרושים תבאו אל־מלכות השמים

Concerning verse 17, Lindsey says:

When Jesus stated that he had come not to "destroy the Law and the Prophets but to strengthen them" (Matthew 5:17) he said that not "one jot or tittle would pass away from the Law until heaven and earth pass away." using as he did so a rabbinic hyperbole which referred to the smallest letter of the Hebrew alphabet and its little hook on the end of the letter.

David Flusser comments on this passage by saying, "Jesus simply intended to say, 'Think not that I come to cancel the law; I do not come to cancel, but to uphold it.'"[227]

Thus according to Flusser, this passage, which is formulaic, phrased the customary language of Jesus' day. In Zephaniah 3:4 the text reads: *Her prophets are light and treacherous persons: her priests have polluted the sanctuary, they have done violence to the law.* In this passage, "to do violence to the law" is to misinterpret the law, and to misinterpret the law is to destroy the law. To do violence or to destroy the law was thus a concept well known and understood by the people during the time of Jesus. That this concept rhetoric is attributed to his preaching places Jesus carefully within the tradition of dissent and resistance to Hellenization that has been traced all along. He identifies with the Jewish community, not as a person trying to destroy it, or to modify its premises, but rather as a leader to take the essence of that community into a new year.

Bivin and Blizzard further illustrate this point in another way when they cite the mistakes modern scholars make as they attempt to exegete this passage. One of the most common mistakes made by Christians is to interpret Matthew 5:17 as meaning, "to abolish or suspend," thus making what Jesus came to do into a break with Hebrew tradition. In this strategy of reading, Romans 10:4, "Christ is the end of the Law," is also used as a proof text to support their position. From a point of view already pursued, the question that needs to be asked is, Did Paul intend Romans 10:4 to be understood as a supporting text proclaiming that the law has been abolished? The answer to this question is a decisive No! It is important to note, however, a supplement to this argument in Matthew 5:17 is Marcion, covered in an earlier chapter, who stated "and his disciples taught a similar approach to the law and the prophets."[228] Concerning this statement, Brad Young writes:

> The church historian E. C. Blackman observed that Marcion and his disciples "undoubtedly adopted Mt. 5:17, after inverting the order of the clauses so as to give exactly an opposite sense." According to their Bible, Jesus taught, "Think not that I have come to fulfill the law, I have not come to fulfill but to abolish." While few modern Christians would resort to changing the words of their Bible, they interpret the words of Jesus in a way that upholds their understanding of a sharp contrast between law and grace. Prejudiced exegesis can have the same result as altering the abolished Jewish law, which brought judgment. On the contrary, the Jewish understanding of Torah encompasses all that is known about God's grace. Divine grace is revealed in Torah. Torah and its deeper revelation of divine mercy and grace, however, are not always interpreted properly. As Christians, we must view the law through the eyes of Jesus. Marcion certainly

did not share Jesus' attitude toward the Judaism of his day. Neither did he share Paul's views, despite the fact that he claimed to be a disciple of Paul. Instead of seeing Torah and the prophets through the eyes of Jesus, Marcion sought to change the meaning of Jesus' teachings and to convert Paul's message into an anti-Jewish gospel.[229]

Modern scholars recognized the error of Marcion influence. They on the other hand, in contrast to Hellenized Christian scholars, emphasized the word "fulfill" in Matthew 5:17. According to Bivin and Blizzard, modern day commentators must take a more measured view of how Jesus' message was weighted in its original context, not as later commentators swayed it. More neutrally, the Jewish Christians of Jesus' era believed "something was lacking in the Law. Jesus completed or fulfilled the Law. He did not do away with the Law. He simply filled up what was lacking."[230]

Not surprisingly, a closer look at this verse from its Hebraic roots reveals something different from that of modern commentators, one that summarizes the case made throughout this text. Let it stand as an example of how a text from that era needs to be considered. First, the passage states, *Think not that I am come or I have come.* The key to the phrase is grammatical. The phrase "I have come" is idiomatic in Hebrew. The phrase is also used in Luke 12:49, *I am (have) come to send fire on the earth.* The word "come" is problematic in that, in the Greek text the verb "come" (*elthon*) is in the aorist tense, and the Greek aorist tense conveys a simple action in the past. In contrast, the Hebrew meaning under the Greek denotes intention or purpose as in "*I intend* to cast fire upon the earth" or "*My purpose* is to cast fire upon the earth." It is clear, therefore, Jesus did not use "I have come" in both Luke and Matthew in the same manner Greek translators rendered this phrase.

The grammar and rhetoric of the phrase had a different meaning during this time than it does today. The cultural and historical conditions of this time should have led each informed commentator to consider the historical situations involved in the text. The Greek and English readings of this text suggest a theological teaching, one which emerges approximately as an interpretation that "immediately pictures Jesus leaving his heavenly throne and, as the Servant of the Lord, coming to earth."[231] Here again, the ultimate interpretation of the passages hangs on the question of what kind of teacher or prophet Jesus is intended to be. And as we have seen, "when Jesus says 'I have come,' he is not referring to his Incarnation."[232] According to Bivin and Blizzard:

> Undoubtedly, in trying to understand this passage, everything hinges on the meaning of the words "destroy" and "fulfill" in verse 17. What does Jesus mean by "destroy the Law" and "fulfill the Law?" "Destroy" and "fulfill" are technical terms used in rabbinic argumentation. When a sage felt that a colleague had misinterpreted a passage of Scripture, he would say, "You are destroying the Law!" Needless to say, in most cases his colleague strongly disagreed. What was "destroying the Law" for one sage, was "fulfilling the Law" (correctly interpreting Scripture) for another.
>
> What we see in Matthew 5:17ff. is a rabbinic discussion. Someone has accused Jesus of "destroying" the Law. Of course, neither Jesus nor his accuser would ever think of literally destroying the Law. Furthermore, it would never enter the accuser's mind to charge Jesus with intent to abolish part or all of the Mosaic Law. What is

being called into question is Jesus' system of interpretation, the way he interprets Scripture. When accused, Jesus strongly denies that his method of interpreting Scripture "destroys" or weakens its meaning. He claims, on the contrary, to be more orthodox than his accuser, For Jesus, a "light" commandment ("Do not bear hatred in your heart") is as important as a "heavy" commandment ("Do not murder"). And a disciple who breaks even a "light" commandment will be considered "light" (having an inferior position) in Jesus' movement (Matthew 5:19).[233]

Here, Bivin and Blizzard take a methodologically necessary step in their reading of this passage. They place Jesus clearly in a Hebraic culture among the sages and rabbis of his day, as Jesus gives his interpretation of his intent or his task concerning the law. Interpreters of the Hellenized Christian traditions have taken this statement as revolution. In doing so it fits their overall preference for a Christianity that has broken with Jewish roots. However, it is truly a statement solidly positioned within the tradition of the Hebrew Scriptures. The text in Zephaniah 3:4 speaks of the polluting of the sanctuary and doing violence to the Law/Torah. In the rabbinic tradition to destroy the Law is equal to doing violence to the Law.

The consistent slant in the translations and interpretations is maintained in most commentaries. In verse 20, for instance, modern commentators compare degrees of righteousness among the religious observant, the Scribes and Pharisees to that of the followers of Christ who are trying to get into heaven. The key to this passage is the understanding of the words "righteousness" and "Kingdom of Heaven." In Matthew 5:6, righteousness denotes "redemption, vindication, salvation, and deliverance."

However, by the time of Jesus, this word had come to mean almsgiving (monetary help to the poor). In the eyes of the Pharisees, almsgiving, prayer, and fasting were the three most important components of righteous living. Almsgiving was the most important of the three, and so synonymous with righteousness, that in time, it (almsgiving) came to be called 'righteousness.'"[234] According to Bivin and Blizzard, Jesus is making a consistent play on these two concepts or meanings. On the one hand *tsedakah* embraces the older, broader meaning of the term, including overtones of "redemption" and or "vindication." In contrast the newer meaning of the word was narrower in scope, which carried the more straightforward, everyday meaning of "almsgiving." Bivin and Blizzard illustrated this point in these words:

> In Jesus' day almsgiving had become a meritorious deed in some circles. Many Jews, like many Christians today, believed they could work out their own righteousness instead of submitting to the righteousness of God (Romans 10:3). But Jesus said: "If your *tsedakah* is not bigger than the *tsedakah* of the scribes and Pharisees – in other words, if it is the undersized *tsedakah* of which the prophets spoke – then you will not get into the Kingdom of Heaven."[235]

Here again, a Greek text is only the thinnest veneer for a set of concepts and actions that can be considered completely representative of major debates within the Hebraic framework of the age.

Without a doubt, then, Semitic sources are the most valuable tools we have for rediscovering the words of Jesus in ways that have not been done before. In *The Sacrifice of Isaac*, Eli Yassif writes "without the help of Jewish exegesis it is impossible to perceive any Christian teaching in its true perspective."[236] Thus, there is a call echoing throughout Biblical academia for the return to Jewish sources as a method of critical studies in the New Testament, a call supported by suggestions on how the cultural and theological politics of interpretation have intervened in investigations of the Bible, which do not consider it a translation in the sense outlined by Lefevere, as described alone.

C. F. Evans, in *The Cambridge History of the Bible*, reinforces my belief in the necessity of this methodological advance by stating:

> Since the Christian *kerugma* was first formulated by Jews for Jews, using Jewish arguments and methods of exposition, it goes without saying that thorough knowledge of contemporary Jewish exegesis is essential to the understanding (and not just a better understanding) of the message of the New Testament and, even more, of Jesus.[237]

For that reason, this text has focused on establishing that there was an original Hebrew text that was beneath the Greek text. It has argued that Semitic sources are without a doubt the key to understanding the Gospels as translations of original community and religious arguments into various political and theological contexts far removed from the originals. By considering the source materials as they have been recovered in new sources, especially the Dead Sea Scrolls, a new generation of Bible scholars follows this example, remembering that parallel to the Hellenistic culture and history, there was a Semitic culture which produced historical sources such as the Dead Sea Scrolls, the Mishnah, the Midrash, and many other valuable sources that open up fascinating new avenues for biblical research.

A clear example of what this study has taught was reflected in the Greek interpretation of the Beatitudes, and how using Greek commentaries to understand the words of Jesus can in many cases produce weak and unproductive interpretations. While on the other hand using the Semitic mythological approach will produce a clearer and more original understanding of the text. Thus in using this Hebraic format, one notices that each Beatitude builds upon each other, because they are all parallel one to another. This is important for the reader, because they show how Jesus used a Semitic style of teaching known as *remez* or hinting. In this teaching style, Jesus hints back to Old Testament passages that were well known to his listeners. The results of not understanding the natural roots of the Gospels can be seen in today's modern commentaries; they misinterpret these important teachings found in the Gospels. However, it is clear that the Hellenized Greek interpretations of the words of Jesus do not just fall short of their true purpose. They, according to the words of Jesus (Matthew 5:17), do violence to the text.

It is also important to note, that this text was not written to disprove the Greek text. It was written to establish that the Hebraic perspective is imperative for our overall learning process of the Biblical text. Greek without Hebrew is just as incomplete as Hebrew without Greek; both contributed to the historical development of our faith. It is my desire that both Greek and Hebrew scholarship meet in that common ground we call the Bible, as researchers work together to unlock the mysteries of Christ's teachings. Then and only then will we begin to become that precious people unto God (I Peter 2:4).

APPENDIX

William Sanford LaSor

William Sanford LaSor, an internationally recognized Semiticist and author with a working knowledge of 20 languages, died January 18, 1991. LaSor was Professor Emeritus of Old Testament at Fuller Theological Seminary. He was Associate Editor of *Biblical Archaeology and Geography, International Standard Bible Encyclopedia, 1961-1988*, the author of 17 books including several on The Dead Sea Scrolls and biblical Greek and Hebrew. He also wrote several hundred articles and was a member of The Society of Old Testament Scholars, the international Organization of Scholars of the Old Testament. A World War II Navy chaplain, LaSor devoted his life to the Bible, seeing it as "our source of morality and hope," as he wrote in the anthology, *Contemporary Authors*. He held six degrees, ranging from chemistry to Oriental Languages and literature, including a doctorate in theology. Born in Philadelphia and ordained in the United Presbyterian Church, he served as a pastor at churches in New Jersey and Pennsylvania before the war and joined Fuller as an associate professor in 1949.

Robert L. Lindsey

Robert L. Lindsey was born in 1917. Dr. Lindsey studied classical Greek as a major at the University of Oklahoma, B.A. In 1939 he traveled to Jerusalem to study Modern and Biblical Hebrew. Upon his return to the United States he completed a Master of Theology degree at Southern Baptist Theological Seminary in Louisville, Kentucky, and a second Master of Theology at Princeton Theological Seminary. He received a Doctorate of Philosophy, also at the Southern Baptist Theological Seminary. Dr. Lindsey was the long-time pastor of Jerusalem's Narkis Street Baptist Congregation. His research on the Synoptic Gospels led to the creation of the Jerusalem School of Synoptic Research. Lindsey's publications include his three-volume *A Comparative Greek Concordance of the Synoptic Gospels*, *A Hebrew Translation of the Gospel of Mark*, *Jesus Rabbi & Lord: The Hebrew Story of Jesus Behind Our Gospels*, and *The Jesus Sources: Understanding the Gospels*.

David Flusser

Professor David Flusser died and was buried in Jerusalem on Friday, September 15, 2000, his 83rd birthday. A founding member of the Jerusalem School of Synoptic Research, Flusser was one of the world's leading Jewish authorities on Early Christianity. His pioneering research on Jesus and Christianity's relationship to Judaism won his international recognition. His collaboration with Robert Lindsey began in 1961 and inspired a new approach to the Synoptic gospels.

Flusser was born in Vienna, but because of food shortages caused by the First World War, his family relocated to the small Catholic Bohemian town of Pribram, Czechoslovakia. As a young man Flusser studied at the University of Prague. On the eve of World War II, Flusser left his native Eastern Europe for the Middle East. He arrived in Palestine in 1939. In 1957 he received his doctorate from the Hebrew University of Jerusalem, where he later taught in the Comparative Religions department for many years. A member of the Israel Academy of Sciences and Humanities, Flusser was frequently recognized for his scholarship: he was awarded the Israel Prize (1980), the State of Israel's most prestigious honor, as well as the Rothschild Prize for Jewish Sciences (2000). He was a recipient of honorary doctorates from, among others, the Catholic Faculty of Theology of Lucerne, Switzerland (1988). Paradoxically, his book *Jesus* has been translated into eleven languages, but not into Hebrew.

Shmuel Safrai

Shmuel Safrai, one of the senior members of the Jerusalem School, is professor of Jewish History of the Mishnaic and Talmudic Period at the Hebrew University. Safrai was born in Warsaw in 1919, and at the age of three immigrated to Palestine with his family. He was ordained as a rabbi at the age of twenty at the prestigious Mercaz Harav Yeshivah in Jerusalem. He later received his M.A. and Ph.D. from the Hebrew University in the fields of Jewish History, Talmud and Bible. He has written twelve books and over eighty articles, and has received many literary prizes for his research, including the 1986 Jerusalem Prize. His publications include, *Pilgrimage in the Period of the Second Temple* (Hebrew), *Rabbi Akiva ben Yosef: His Life and Teaching* (Hebrew), *The Jewish People in the First Century*, co-editor (2 vols.), and *The Literature of the Sages, Part I*, editor.

Roy B. Blizzard, Jr.

Roy B. Blizzard, Jr., was for several years (1968-1974) an instructor in the Hebrew Studies Program at the University of Texas at Austin, and later served as an Adjunct Assistant Professor in The Center for Middle Eastern Studies. A native of Joplin Missouri, Dr. Blizzard attended Oklahoma Military Academy and has a B.A. degree from Phillips University in Enid, Oklahoma. He has a M.A. from Eastern New Mexico University in Portales, New Mexico, a M.A. from the University of Texas at Austin, and a Ph.D. in Hebrew Studies from the University of Texas at Austin.

Dr. Blizzard studied at the Hebrew University in Jerusalem, Israel in the summer of 1966. In the summer of 1973, Dr. Blizzard worked on the archaeological excavations at Tel Qasile where a Philistine Temple dating from 1200 B.C. was excavated. In 1968, 1971, and 1972, he worked on the excavations at the Western Wall at the Temple Mount in Jerusalem. Since then much of his time has been spent in Israel and the Middle East in study and research. Dr. Blizzard has directed numerous Historical Archaeological Study Seminars to Israel, Jordan, Egypt, Turkey, Greece, and Italy. He is the author of *The Bible Sex and You*, *Mishnah and the Words of Jesus*, *Tithing Giving and Prosperity*, *The Mountain of the Lord*, *Understanding the Difficult Words of Jesus* (with David Bivin), and numerous articles.

Marvin R. Wilson

Marvin R. Wilson is the Harold J. Ockenga Professor of Biblical and Theological Studies at Gordon College, Wenham, Massachusetts. He has been honored two times at Gordon commencements with the senior faculty award for "Excellence in Teaching." His field-trip course at Gordon, titled "Modern Jewish Culture," is cited as an educational model in the field of interfaith relations. Wilson has authored or edited seven books and also penned numerous articles in both scholarly and popular periodicals. Four of his books deal with the relationship between Christianity and Judaism. His most recent work, *Our Father Abraham: Jewish Roots of the Christian Faith*, is a textbook on the Hebrew heritage of the church. Wilson served as an Old Testament translator and editor on *The New International Version*, and contributed notes to books in the *NIV Study Bible*.

Brad H. Young

Brad H. Young is the founder and president of the Gospel Research Foundation, Tulsa Oklahoma. A founding member of the Jerusalem School of Synoptic Research, he is professor of Biblical Literature in the Graduate School of Theology and Ministry at Oral Roberts University. Young earned M.A. and Ph.D. degrees in Judaism and Early Christianity at the Hebrew University, Jerusalem, Israel, where he studied for ten years. His doctoral dissertation was written under the supervision of Professor David Flusser, and published by Paulist Press titled *Jesus and His Jewish Parables: Rediscovering the Roots of Jesus' Teaching*. Young has also authored several other texts, *The Jewish Background to the Lord's Prayer*, *The Parables: Jewish Tradition and Christian Interpretation*, *Jesus the Jewish Theologian*, *Paul the Jewish Theologian*, and *Meet the Rabbis*.

David Bivin

David Bivin is a member of the Jerusalem School of Synoptic Research, a think tank made up of Jewish and Christian scholars dedicated to better understanding the Synoptic Gospels (Matthew, Mark, and Luke). In the early 1980s, before the School became a legal entity, he coined its name. For most of the years since 1985, when the School was registered in Israel as a nonprofit research institute, David served as the School's director and chairman of its Executive Board.

A native of Cleveland, Oklahoma, David has lived in Israel since 1963, when he came to Jerusalem on a Rotary Foundation Fellowship to do postgraduate work at the Hebrew University. He remained at the Hebrew University until 1969 studying Jewish history and literature under professors Menahem Stern, David Flusser, Shmuel Safrai, and Yechezkel Kutscher, and studied archaeology under professors Yigael Yadin, Yohanan Ahoroni, and Michael Avi-Yonah. During those six years, and for many years afterwards, he also studied privately with Jerusalem scholar-pastor Robert L. Lindsey. David is the co-founder of the Jerusalem Perspective.

BIBLIOGRAPHY

Aland, Kurt, and Barbara Aland. *The Greek New Testament.* Stuttgart: Deutsche Bibelgesellschaft/The United Bible Societies, 1966.

Aland, Kurt. *A History of Christianity.* Philadelphia: Fortress Press, 1980.

Aland, Kurt, ed. *Synopsis of the Four Gospels.* 6th rev. ed. Stuttgart: Deutsche Bibelgescllschaft/United Bible Society, 1983.

Albright, W.F. "Archaeological Discovery and the Scriptures," *Christianity Today,* Vol. XII, No. 19 (June 21, 1968): 3-5.

Albright, W.F., and C.S. Mann. *Matthew.* Vol. 1 of *The Anchor Bible.* New York Doubleday, 1971.

Avi-Yonah, M. *The Jews under Roman and Byzantine Rule,* Jerusalem: The Magnes Press, The Hebrew University, 1984.

Bauer, Walter, William F. Arndt, and F. Wilbur Gingrich. *A Greek-English Lexicon of The New Testament.* London: University of Chicago Press, 1958.

Bivin, David, and Roy Blizzard, Jr. *Understanding the Difficult Words of Jesus: New Insights From a Hebraic Perspective*. Dayton, Ohio: Center for Judaic-Christian Studies, 1994.

Blackman, Philip. *Order Zeraim*. Vol. I or *Mishnayoth*. Gateshead, Germany: Judaic Press, Ltd., 1993.

Blackman, Philip. *Order Moed*. Vol. II of *Mishnayoth*. Gateshead, Germany: Judaic Press, Ltd., 1993.

Blackman, Philip. *Order Nezikin*. Vol. IV of *Mishnayoth*. Gateshead, Germany: Judaic Press, Ltd., 1993.

Braude, William, G. (Gershon Zev): *Tanna Debe Eliyyahu: The Lore of the School of Elijah*. Philadelphia: The Jewish Publication Society of America. 1981.

Buchler, Adolf. *Studies in Sin and Atonement in the Rabbinic Literature of the First Century*, London: Humpherey Milford, Oxford University Press, 1928.

Buchler, Adolf. *Types of Jewish-Palestinian Piety: The Ancient Pious Men*. New York: KTAV Publishing House, Inc. 1968.

Crombie, Frederick, and William Stewart. *Critical and Exegetical Hand-Book to the Gospel of Matthew*. New York: Funk & Wagnalls, 1884.

Cross, Frank Moore, and Shemaryahu Tallmon. *Qumran and the History of the Biblical Text*. Cambridge, Massachusetts: Harvard University Press, 1975.

Danby, Herbert, and Elijah ben Solomon. *The Mishnah*. Oxford: Oxford University Press, 1938.

Davies, William David, and Dale C. Allison, Jr., *A Critical and Exegetical Commentary on the Gospel According to Saint Matthew*. Vol. I. Edinburgh: T. & T. Clark Limited, 1988.

Delitzsch, Franz, trans. *The New Testament In Hebrew and English*. Cambridge: Society for Distributing Hebrew Scriptures, n.d.

Eisenman, Robert. *James the Brother of Jesus*. New York: The Penguin Group, 1997.

Epstein, I. (Rabbi). *The Babylonian Talmud. Seder Zera'im*, London: The Soncino Press, 1958.

Epstein, I. (Rabbi). *Sanhedrin: Hebrew-English Edition of the Babylonian Talmud*. London: The Soncino Press, 1987.

Evans, C. F. *The Cambridge History of the Bible*. Vol. I. Cambridge: University Press, 1970.

Feuerbach, Ludwig. *The Essence of Christianity*. New York: Prometheus Books, 1989.

Finkelstein, Louis, and Saul Horowitz. *Sifre Devarim*. New York: Jewish Theological Seminary, 1960.

Flusser, David. *Jesus*. Jerusalem: The Magnes Press, The Hebrew University, 1997.

Flusser, David. *Jewish Sources in Early Christianity*. New York: Adama Books, 1987.

Frankovic, Joseph. *The Kingdom of Heaven*. Tulsa, OK: HaKesher, Inc. 1998.

Fredriksen, Paula. *Jesus of Nazareth, King of the Jews*. New York: Vintage Books/Random House, Inc. 1999.

Freedman, David Noel, ed. *The Anchor Bible Dictionary*. Vol. IV. New York: Doubleday, 1922.

Gaster, Theodor H. *The Dead Sea Scriptures*. New York: Anchor Books, 1956.

Gesenius, Wilhelm, Emil Kautzsch, and Arthur Ernst Cowley. *Gesenius' Hebrew Grammar*. 2d ed. Oxford: Clarendon Press, 1910.

Goodman, Philip. *The Rosh Hashanah Anthology*. Philadelphia: The Jewish Publication Society of America, 1970.

Hagner, Donald A. *World Biblical Commentary: Matthew 1-13. Vol. 33a*, Dallas, Texas: Word Books, Publisher, 1993.

Hammer, Reuven. *Sifre: A Tannaitic Commentary on the Book of Deuteronomy*. New Haven and London: Yale University Press, 1986.

Hare, Douglas R. *Matthew: Interpretation*. Louisville: John Knox Press, 1946.

Hatch, Edwin, and Henry A. Redpath. *A Concordance to the Septuagint*. Vol. I: A-I. Grand Rapids, MI: Baker Book House, 1983.

Hatch, Edwin, and Henry A. Redpath. *A Concordance to the Septuagint*. Vol. II: K-S. Grand Rapids, MI: Baker Book House, 1983.

Hertz, Joseph H. *The Authorized Daily Prayer Book*. New York: Bloch Publishing Company, 1965.

Hester, H. I. *The Heart of Hebrew History: A Study of the Old Testament*. Liberty, MO: The Quality Press, Inc. 1962.

Hewett, James Allen. *New Testament Greek: A Beginning and Intermediate Grammar*. Peabody, MA: Hendrickson Publishers, 1986.

Horovitz, H. S., ed. *Sifra: Al Bemidbar Vesifre Zuta*. Jerusalem: Wahramaan, 1966.

Kadushin, Max. *A Conceptual Approach to the Mekilta*. New York: The Jewish Theological Seminary, 1969.

Kadushin, Max. *Organic Thinking: A Study in Rabbinic Thought*. New York: The Jewish Theological Seminary of America, 1938.

Kadushin, Max. *The Rabbinic Mind*. New York: Bloch Publishing Company, 1972.

Keener, Craig S. *A Commentary on the Gospel of Matthew*. Grand Rapids, MI: William B. Eerdmans Publishing Company, 1960.

Kilpatrick, G. D. *The Origins of the Gospel According to St. Matthew*. Oxford: At The Clarendon Press, 1946.

Koester, Helmut. *Introduction to the New Testament: History, Culture, and Religion of the Hellenistic Age*. Vol. I. Berlin: Walter De Gruyter, 1982.

Kohler, Kaufmann. *Jewish Theology, Systematically and Historically Considered*. New York: The Macmillan Company, 1981.

Lachs, Samuel Tobias. *A Rabbinic Commentary on the New Testament: The Gospels of Matthew, Mark and Luke.* Hoboken, NJ: KTAV Publishing House, Inc., 1987.

Lamm, Norman. *The Shema: Spirituality and Law in Judaism.* Philadelphia: The Jewish Publication Society, 1998.

Lange, John Peter. *Commentary on the Holy Scriptures,* Grand Rapids, MI: Zondervan Publishing House, 1882.

Lauterbach, Jocob Z. *Mekilta De-Rabbi Ishmael.* Vol. I. Philadelphia: The Jewish Publication Society of America, 1933.

Lauterbach, Jacob Z. *Mekilta De-Rabbi Ishmael.* Vol. II. Philadelphia: The Jewish Publication Society of America, 1933.

Lefevere, Andre. *Translating Literature: Practice and Theory in a Comparative Literature Context.* New York: Modern Language Association of America, 1992.

Lehrman, Simon M. (Rabbi). *Midrash Rabbah: Exodus.* London, New York: The Soncino Press, 1983.

Lindsey, Robert L. *A Hebrew Translation of the Gospel of Mark.* Jerusalem: Dugith Publisher Baptist House, 1969.

Lindsey, Robert L. *Jesus Rabbi and Lord: The Hebrew Story of Jesus Behind Our Gospels.* Oak Creek, WI: Cornerstone Publishing, 1990.

Metzger, Bruce M. ed. *The Apocrypha: The Oxford Annotated Apocrypha.* New York: Oxford University Press, 1977.

Montefiore, Claude G. and Herbert M. J. Loewe. *A Rabbinic Anthology.* New York: Schocken Books, 1974.

Moore, George Foot. *Judaism in the First Centuries of the Christian era: The Age of Tannaim.* Vol. II. New York: Schocken Books, 1932.

Neusner, Jacob. *Christianity, Judaism and Other Greco-Roman Cults.* Netherland: E. J. Brill, 1975.

Neusner, Jacob, and Bruce Chilton. *Jewish-Christian Debates: God, Kingdom, Messiah.* Minneapolis: Fortress Press, 1971.

Neusner, Jacob, trans. *Sifra: An Analytical Translation.* Vol. III. Atlanta: Scholars Press, 1988.

Pasachoff, Naomi and Robert J. Littman. *Jewish History in 100 Nutshells.* London: Jason Aronson Inc, 1943.

Pococke, Edward. *A Commentary on the Prophecy of Micah.* England: Oxford, 1676.

Safrai, Shmuel. *Spoken Languages in the Time of Jesus.* Jerusalem: Jerusalem Perspective, n.d.

Sanders, E. P. *Jesus and Judaism.* Philadelphia: Fortress Press, 1985.

Santala, Risto. *The Messiah in the New Testament in the Light of Rabbinical Writings.* Jerusalem: Keren Ahvah Meshihit, 1992.

Schaff, Philip. *History of the Christian Church.* Vol. I. Grand Rapids, MI: Wm. B. Eerdmans Publishing Company, 1910.

Schaff, Philip. *History of the Christian Church.* Vol. II. Grand Rapids, MI: Wm. B. Eerdmans Publishing Company, 1910.

Schaff, Philip. *History of the Christian Church.* Vol. III. Grand Rapids, MI: Wm. B. Eerdmans Publishing Company, 1910.

Schaff, Philip. *History of the Christian Church.* Vol. IV. Grand Rapids, MI: Wm. B. Eerdmans Publishing Company, 1910.

Schechter, Solomon. *Aspects of Rabbinic Theology : Major Concepts of the Talmud.* New York: Schocken Books, 1909.

Schechter, Solomon. *The Jewish Quarterly Review.* Special Issue: Rabbinic Parallels to the New Testament, Vol. 12, 1966.

Shanks, Herschel. *Christianity and Rabbinic Judaism: A Parallel History of Their Origins and Early Development.* Washington, D.C.: Biblical Archaeology Society, 1992.

Shinan, Avigdor, ed., *Midrash Shmuel.* Jerusalem: Hillel Press, 1984.

Sparks, Hedley Frederick Davis. *The Apocryphal Old Testament*. Oxford: Clarendon, 1987.

Strauss, David Friedrich. *The Life of Jesus Critically Examined*. Philadelphia: Fortress Press, 1972.

Talmud Jerusalem. Krotoshin Edition. Jerusalem: Hillel Press, 1982.

Tanna Debe Eliyyahu, *Eliyyahu Zuta*. Philadelphia: Jewish Publication Society, 1975.

Trapp, John. *A Commentary on the Old and New Testaments*. Vol. Five. Eureka, CA: Tanski Publications, 1997.

Urbach, Ephraim E. *The Sages: Their Concepts and Beliefs*. Cambridge, MA: Harvard University Press, 1987.

Wilson, Marvin R. *Our Father Abraham: Jewish Roots of the Christian Faith*. Grand Rapids, MI: William B. Eerdmans Publishing Company, 1989.

Yassif, Eli. *The Sacrifice of Isaac: Studies in the Development of a Literary Tradition*. Jerusalem: Makor Publishing, Ltd., n.d.

Yeager, Randolph O. *The Renaissance New Testament. Vol. I*. Bowling Green, KY: Renaissance Press, Inc. 1976.

Young, Brad H. "Dead Sea Scrolls Conference." *Yavo Digest* (Austin, TX.), Vol. VII. Number 2, (1993): 17.

Young, Brad H. "The Dead Sea Scrolls Deception." *Yavo Digest* (Austin, TX.), Vol. VI. Number 2, (1992): 18.

Young, Brad H. *Jesus and His Jewish Parables: Rediscovering the Roots of Jesus' Teaching*. New York: Paulist Press, 1989.

Young, Brad H. *Jesus The Jewish Theologian*. Peabody, MA: Hendrickson Publishers, Inc. 1995.

Young, Brad H. *The Parables: Jewish Tradition and Christian Interpretation*. Peabody, MA: Hendrickson Publishers, Inc. 1998.

Young, Brad H. *Paul, The Jewish Theologian: A Pharisee among Christians, Jews, and Gentiles*. Peabody, MA: Hendrickson Publishers, Inc. 1997.

ABOUT THE AUTHOR

 Dr. William V. McDonald is president of New Life Teaching Center, New Life Ministries, Inc. Based in Austin, TX, the organization is dedicated to bible research and education. He is an Associate Professor in the graduate School of Theology and Mission at Oral Roberts University since 2002 – teaching Old Testament/Hebrew Scriptures courses. Dr. McDonald has over 30 years of experience in educational ministry teachings.

Dr. McDonald received a Ph.D. in Hebrew Studies from the University of Texas at Austin in 2002. He holds Master of Divinity (1991), and Master of Arts in Biblical Literature degrees (1992) from Oral Roberts University, and a Masters degree in Hebrew Studies from the University of Texas at Austin (1999).

Dr. McDonald hosts a national weekly television show, *On Wings of Truth*, which airs on Gods Learning Channel (GLC) cable network. Over the past 30 years, he has taught and hosted numerous television outreach programs including *Truth Ministries* in Peoria, IL and *The Quest* in Austin, TX. He hosted and taught two television programs produced by NLM Foundation for Depression and Anxiety, entitled *Overcoming Depression, Anxiety and Worry* and *Face To Face, a biblical study to understand human behavior.*

In addition to *A Hebrew Text in Greek Dress,* he is the author of *You Are Free to Worry No More.* He has written a number of articles published by Yavo Digest in Austin, TX. and Not Forsaking the Assembling (NFTA).

Dr. McDonald was a member of the Board of Directors of the American Forum for Jewish-Christian Cooperation where he served as National Director of Race Relations (1987-1994).

ALSO BY WILLIAM V. MCDONALD

You Are Free to Worry No More

www.wmcdonaldministry.com

New Life Teaching Center, New Life Ministries, Inc.
Austin, Texas

CPSIA information can be obtained at www.ICGtesting.com
Printed in the USA
LVOW12s0051051214

417224LV00001BA/14/P

9 781500 923518